DATE DUE

OCT 0 6 2000	
OCT 2 7 2000	
DEC 1 6 2001	

GAYLORD   PRINTED IN U.S.A.

The World and Warren's Cartoons

BOOKS BY WALTER CONSUELO LANGSAM
The World and Warren's Cartoons
Where Freedom Exists
World History Since 1870
Historic Documents of World War II
Franz der Gute: Die Jugend eines Kaisers
The World Since 1919
Francis the Good: the Education of an Emperor (1768-1792)
A Narrative of War
Documents and Readings in the History of Europe Since 1918
In Quest of Empire: the Problem of Colonies
Major European and Asiatic Developments Since 1935
The World Since 1914
The Napoleonic Wars and German Nationalism in Austria

THE WORLD AND
WARREN'S CARTOONS

Walter Consuelo Langsam, Ph.D., LL.D.
President Emeritus, University of Cincinnati

AN EXPOSITION-BANNER BOOK

Exposition Press   *Hicksville, New York*

All the cartoons in this book have been reprinted with the kind permission of the *Cincinnati Enquirer*

CONTENTS

PREFACE

One evening, at a pleasant social gathering, we found ourselves expressing admiration, respectively, for one another's professional work. Walter C. Langsam spoke of the artistry, wit, and cogency of L. D. Warren's nationally syndicated cartoons in the *Cincinnati Enquirer;* Warren mentioned how very readable he thought were Langsam's history books, particularly the eight editions of *The World Since 1919,* published by the MacMillan Company.

Out of the friendly exchange, grew this project of collaboration on a short, popular history of the major powers since the end of World War II, accompanied by a selection of Warren's most effective cartoons (reprinted with the permission of the *Cincinnati Enquirer*). The words "accompanied by" are used advisedly, since the text within each chapter is paralleled by what in effect is a series of lively picture-stories covering the same events.

For the sake of interest, the opening chapter describes briefly the development of cartooning and contains a biographical sketch of Warren as one of the country's leading editorial cartoonists. An Appendix, graciously provided by Art Wood, Jr., of Washington, D.C., summarizes for the first time in print the history of the highly regarded Association of American Editorial Cartoonists, since its founding in 1957.

We hope the public may find as much pleasure in perusing the volume as we did in writing and compiling it.

Cincinnati　　　　　　　　　　　　　　　　WALTER C. LANGSAM
June, 1976　　　　　　　　　　　　　　　　L. D. WARREN

The World and Warren's Cartoons

1

CARTOONS:
"THE MOST PENETRATING
OF CRITICISMS"

"Them Damn Pictures"

The origin of the cartoon as a medium of visual communication has been placed variously in prehistoric, ancient, medieval, and modern times—depending largely on the writer's interpretation or definition of the word! Perhaps the most practical approach to dating is to think in terms of a chronologically overlapping development from primitive times to the present.

The progression then may be traced broadly as follows: prehistoric pictorial representations on cave walls and on leather; caricatures on stone slabs, on woodcuts, and, eventually, on printed paper; satirical chiselings or drawings on stone, walls, paper, and cardboard; social and political cartoons on flyers, posters, and the printed page; and, finally, the editorial cartoon.* In each of these categories, it was and is the aim of the artist to provide a picture-story selected from life. In early times, the selections were from life nearby; later, from life both at home and abroad.

The prehistoric cave drawings and leather scrapings in Europe, the Asian Indian and Far Eastern stone carvings, the American Indian leather painting and beading, and the like, all were imaginative pictorial expressions or symbols using available media to record observations, or legendary observations, of animals, nature, and everyday life. Aside from such seemingly natural human desires as to describe, to revere, to symbolize, to laugh at, or to express pique, motivation for at least some of these creative manifestations probably lay in the hope of even primitive man somehow to live on after physical death.

---

*Comic strips, humorous depictions such as those in *The New Yorker,* and "animated" drawings of the Walt Disney type popularly also are called cartoons, but it is not with these that we here are concerned.

Interesting examples of very early caricatures and satirical portrayals, involving the poking of fun at others through graphic means, have been found in Egypt and Italy. Thus, there is preserved in the New York Historical Society's collections a humorous Egyptian carving on a limestone slab, dating from the twelfth century B.C.; it shows files of slaves carrying home on their shoulders the supine bodies of their drunken masters after a banquet. And there still exists a Pompeiian drawing from A.D. 79 on a barracks wall, depicting in unflattering stance a military officer; presumably it was done by a soldier under the martinet's command.

During medieval and early modern times, Western Europe saw the gradual development of a technique of exaggerated depiction of individuals or groups that came to be called caricature, from the Italian *caricare,* to "overload" or "overburden." Generally, this form of expression was limited to wordless pictures, although these sometimes did bear labels to identify the characters. Some of the caricatures were humorous and some were gross and even vicious, but always they exaggerated unflatteringly some person's or some group's form and features.

The use of words as captions, descriptions, or dialogue became increasingly widespread after the invention of movable type for printing in the fifteenth century. The flexibility thus provided encouraged the growth of satire as a means of exposing and deriding human folly, vanity, and vices. Some of the early caricatures, particularly in the Germanies and the Netherlands during the time of the Reformation and the Religious Wars in the sixteenth and seventeenth centuries, were of the highest artistic value. A number, indeed, were done by such leading artists of the day as Albrecht Dürer. Caricatures and satirical flyers and posters appeared in profusion during the French Revolutionary and Napoleonic ages, especially in England and France. They began to appear in the American colonies at least as early as the mideighteenth century, and in the United States from its beginning as an independent nation.

According to one authority, William Murrell, the word "cartoon" to designate a picture story was used as far back as 1775. In that year, an English engraving was titled "The Political Cartoon for the Year 1775." But it was not until the midnineteenth century that this use of a word previously meaning a model for a fresco, tapestry, or painting on a *cartone,* from the Italian for "pasteboard," popularly came to replace "caricature" as a term for pictorialized comment on persons and events in newspapers and periodicals.

The later nineteenth and early twentieth centuries witnessed a growing emphasis on social and political cartooning, and the post-World War II years brought with them the regular appearance in many newspapers of the so-called editorial cartoons. These last normally have appeared on the editorial pages of the printed news media. On occasion, however, when the editorial cartoonist's viewpoint and that of the paper's editor have varied widely, the cartoon has been placed on the page facing the editorial one, rather than directly among the editorial columns.

The first use of the name "cartoon," in the modern sense, to capture the public's fancy occurred in July, 1843, in an issue of London's *Punch* magazine. During the previous month, there had been placed on exhibition in Westminster Hall a group of cartoons for frescos, from among which would be selected a number to decorate the Houses of Parliament. Thereupon, in the July 1, 1843, issue of *Punch,* the editors indicated that "Mr. Punch has the benevolence to announce that in an early Number of the present Volume he will astonish the Parliamentary Committee by publication of several exquisite designs, to be called *Punch's Cartoons.*"

The issue of July 15, 1843, then carried "Cartoon No. 1," drawn by John Leech and titled, "Substance and Shadow." The picture sarcastically chided Parliament for offering the country's paupers the "shadow" of an exhibition instead of the "substance" of food and clothing. The cleverness and forcefulness of the drawing evidently appealed to the reading public, and so the word "cartoon" from 1843 onward gradually entered the everyday language of people throughout most of the world.

Almost from the beginning, perhaps, picture stories have proved to be, in the words of Aldous Leonard Huxley, "the most penetrating of criticisms." Generally, the caricatures and cartoons have been restricted in interest, timeliness, and influence. Some of the best, however, that is to say, some of the wittiest or bitterest or cleverest or most vicious or most fundamental in understanding have had universal appeal and achieved historical longevity.

Outstanding modern British cartoonists whose work falls within the lasting category have been, among many others, Sir John Tenniel (1820-1914), Bruce Bairnsfather (1888-1959), and Sir David Low (1891-1963).

Tenniel, who joined the staff of *Punch* in 1850, drew some 2000 cartoons for that magazine. One of the longest remembered of these, still frequently reproduced in history books and biographies, appeared on March 29, 1890, at the time of the aged Chancellor Otto von Bismarck's dismissal by the young German Emperor William II. Entitled "Dropping the Pilot," it showed a somber Bismarck descending the pilot's ladder of a large ship (Germany), across the deck railing of which leaned a smirking William II, with imperial crown askew.

The Scottish Bruce Bairnsfather produced what probably was the most famous cartoon of World War I. It showed two much-battered British soldiers crouching in a hole in France's "No-Man's Land," with the one muttering to the other, "Well, if you knows a better 'ole, go to it."

And Sir David Low so effectively ridiculed Adolf Hitler and the preten-
sions of his Nazi followers that he was said to have been second only to
Sir Winston Churchill on the Nazis' list of foreign "criminals."

The generally accepted first—or at least first politically significant—
American cartoon (aside from satirical caricatures) was the work of
Benjamin Franklin (1706-1790). It was a woodcut picture, published
in the *Pennsylvania Gazette* in 1754, showing the American colonies as
segmented parts of a snake. The caption read: "Join, or Die."

A little more than a century later, came the powerful drawings of the
German-born American cartoonist, Thomas Nast (1840-1902), who,
incidentally, in a drawing of 1886, presented to the world its modern
image of jolly old Santa Claus. From 1870-1872 he so effectively exposed
in cartoons in *Harper's Weekly* the corruption of the Democratic party in
New York (Tammany Hall) as to help drive its chief, William M. "Boss"
Tweed, into foreign flight and eventual imprisonment.

"I don't care what they print about me," Tweed was reported to have
said in 1871, "most of my constituents can't read anyway; but them
damn pictures!" In commenting fifty-five years later on this perception of
Tweed's, Clifford K. Berryman, sometime editorial cartoonist for the
Washington Evening Star, wrote: "There is no doubt that a serious
political issue, when presented in the form of a telling cartoon, will be
borne home to the minds of a far larger circle of average everyday men and
women, than it ever could be when discussed in the cold black and white
of the editorial column."*

In the late 1890's, while Nast was still alive, the perfection of the
photo-engraving process served as a stimulus to the increasingly frequent
appearance of cartoons in the daily press. With opportunity available,
and with recognition given to talent, there then developed, during the
ensuing decades, a corps of outstanding political and editorial cartoonists.
Among many others, these included Homer Davenport of the *New York
Evening Journal,* John T. McCutcheon of the *Chicago Tribune* (which
published his work in color on its front page), Rollin Kirby of the *New York
World,* Jay Norwood "Ding" Darling of the *New York Herald-Tribune,*
Herbert L. Block ("Herblock") of the *Washington Post,* Karl Hubenthal
of the *Los Angeles Herald-Examiner,* John Fischetti of the *Chicago Daily
News,* Paul Conrad of the *Los Angeles Times,* Pat Oliphant of the *Wash-
ington Star,* Don Wright of the *Miami News,* and Jeff MacNelly of the
Richmond News-Leader.

World War II produced America's version of Bruce Bairnsfather in
the young soldier, William Henry "Bill" Mauldin (1921-   ). In the

---

*Clifford K. Berryman, "Development of the Cartoon," in *The University of
Missouri Bulletin,* Vol. 27, No. 22, Journalism Series, No. 41, 1926, p. 19.

"G.I." periodical, *Stars and Stripes,* and later in the syndicated national press, he immortalized the ordinary soldier and his philosophy in striking picture stories of "Willie and Joe." Several years after the war, he joined the *St. Louis Post-Dispatch* as an editorial cartoonist and won a second Pulitzer Prize for his work. A few years later, he was employed by the *Chicago Sun-Times.*

* * *

In speaking of cartooning during the "today" of 1926, Clifford K. Berryman wrote prophetically: "There is nothing in our modern life so alarming as the power which reckless and dissolute talent has to make virtuous life seem provincial and ridiculous, vicious life graceful and metropolitan." More reassuringly, he added, "It is curious to note also that cartoons and caricatures on the wrong side of great public questions are never excellent."*

These wise words tempt one to essay a "profile" of the ideal editorial cartoonist of the today and tomorrow of the second half of the twentieth century. Although one probably would have to search among the archangels to find anyone characterized by all the desirable traits, it yet seems not inappropriate to visualize the paragon as a standard against whom to measure practicing professionals. Certainly some practitioners have been influential even though their work has reflected only few of the qualities enumerated below; in general, however, *their* influence has been of short duration and, in the long view, not conducive to the common weal.

Perhaps the best, certainly the most convenient, source for a study of the responsible editorial cartoonist is the work produced by members of the esteemed Association of American Editorial Cartoonists, founded in 1957.† From such a study, it would seem that first, a good editorial cartoonist must have a lively visual imagination, possess wit, and be a highly skilled draftsman. Apparently formal training in art and painting is not essential, for many of the best-known editorial cartoonists of the 1950s and 1960s had no such instruction. Nor, incidentally, in a perhaps astonishingly large number of cases had they earned a college degree or even attended college.

Regardless of educational background, however, those cartoonists who have enjoyed prolonged popularity and influence have been able to *draw.* This skill marks also the work of a gratifying number of the newer editorial cartoonists who, during the early 1970s, gradually have been

---

*Berryman, *op. cit.,* p. 19.
†See the Appendix for a brief history of this association.

replacing the retiring giants. With growing experience, the best among the successor cartoonists doubtless will produce cartoons characterized by the same degree of subtlety, wit, drafting skill, and imagination that customarily marked the distinguished editorial cartoons of earlier decades.

Further, the study reveals the fact that no picture-story can be clear and telling unless its creator himself is a clear thinker, endowed with common sense. Muddled thought and intellectual confusion are not conducive to the production of sharp, well-focused, universally understood cartoons. Beyond this, clear thinking in the production of editorial cartoons evidently demands a reasonably sound historical perspective. Without such a perspective, it becomes virtually impossible for the cartoonist to sense which topics or events are likely to have more than passing importance, or to attract more than fleeting interest. A sense of history, reinforced by some factual knowledge of how the world "got this way," is basic to an understanding of the major current developments during *any* period, and certainly in the period of today's complex, confused, and confusing world, with its troubled, restless, and insecure humanity.

As might be expected, the works of the acknowledged leaders reflect maturity, and that in many guises. This may be owing, in part, to the circumstance that most of the editorial cartoonists during the quarter-century following World War II already had had considerable experience as general cartoonists, having drawn in a variety of picture-story fields. Too, they had discovered early that long hours and hard work were essential to success here as in most areas of human endeavor.

In any case, and as a group, they clearly seemed to have learned to differentiate between wit and wise-cracking, between moral courage and brashness, between good taste and bad, between idealism and naïveté, between basic and ephemeral causes, and, above all, between integrity in its literal meaning of individual honesty and mere stubbornness or arrogance. They had lived sufficiently long and experienced enough so as to have developed broad human interests and a personal philosophy of life, a philosophy rooted in a recognition of the primacy of eternal values over material and transitory considerations. Possessed of these insights, they, more often than not, could and did successfully illustrate, illuminate, and direct attention to the fundamentals of human life and historical development.

Perhaps another, and briefer, way of saying all this is to note that the ablest and most influential editorial cartoonists have been imbued with, and have manifested in their artistry, a deep sense of responsibility. They have used their talents constructively, being ever mindful of the priceless worth of human dignity. And, where humor has been appropriate, they have exercised in even their most critical displays of wit and fun-poking a gentleness and mellowness that achieved far more and hurt far less than would have a crude and biting "cleverness."

The good editorial cartoonist, in his positive criticism, does not "strip the tree of both caterpillars and blossoms." And since he knows and is willing to acknowledge that faith, hope, love, and hard work underlie continuing success in his chosen profession, he never thinks of it as one "whereby men grow important and formidable at very small expense."*

"L.D." Warren

Outstanding among the responsible editorial cartoonists of the post-World War II era was Leonard D. Warren of Cincinnati. From 1947 until his retirement at the end of 1973, he daily (except Sunday) recorded, in the pages of the *Cincinnati Enquirer,* the then current events in witty, imaginative, profound, and striking pictorial drawings.

Leonard Deakyne Warren, known since high-school days as "L.D.," was born on December 27, 1906, in Wilmington, Delaware, the third of the six children of Robert Leroy Warren and Annie Richardson Melvin Warren. The senior Warren was a meat cutter who, about 1908, moved with his family to Camden, New Jersey, where he eventually came to operate his own butcher shop.

While attending the Reed (Primary) School, Warren saved a small boy from death by drowning, and thus early came to have his name in a newspaper! At the Sewell (Grammar) School, one of his teachers, Miss Elizabeth Stradling, detected and fostered his interest in drawing. In gratitude, L.D. and a similarly talented friend on one occasion gave Miss Stradling a collection of caricatures of all their classmates. His parents, too, encouraged Warren's artistic interest, and proudly pinned the child's drawings to the walls. It was during these formative years, moreover, that he joined a branch of the YMCA and began to develop his later exceptional gymnastic skill.

L.D. enrolled in the college preparatory course at the Camden High School. Too slight in build and short of stature to participate in the traditional team contact sports, he chose to excel in gymnastics and tumbling, activities that he continued to pursue, and in which he continued to star, after graduation from secondary school.† At Camden High, he again had a stimulating and encouraging art teacher, Mrs. Flora Brugger Curtin, and became an active member of the Art Club. On the

---

*The two quotations, taken from remarks on literary criticism, are cited, respectively, from Jean Paul Richter, *Titan,* ca. 1803, and Samuel Johnson, *The Idler,* June 9, 1759.

†Between 1929 and 1934, he won two gold, one silver, and three bronze medals for his gymnastics feats in several New Jersey State Championship and one Middle Atlantic Amateur Athletic Union (AAU) competitions.

outside, he earned money as a newspaper carrier. Surely, all this was an interesting combination of activities for a later professional newspaper cartoonist.

Following graduation from high school in 1925, Warren chose full-time employment rather than college. In his first regular job, he worked as lettering-artist for the Fenton Label Company in Philadelphia. Then, in 1926 and at age twenty, on the basis of submitted art samples, he was appointed to the staff of the independent *Camden Courier Post.* His earliest duties here were to make advertising drawings and provide special feature cartoons. Thus began a newspaper career that was to span forty-eight years of distinguished and influential picture-story telling.

In 1928, J. David Stern, publisher of the *Camden Courier Post,* purchased the *Philadelphia Record,* a leading Democratic newspaper. The art work for both papers now was done in Philadelphia, from where L.D. contributed to both sheets. His assignments henceforth included not merely advertising and sports-cartoon drawings, but feature- and theatre cartoons and original comic strips as well.

Soon Warren became assistant to the *Philadelphia Record*'s well-known editorial cartoonist, Jerry Doyle. Simultaneously, he served as free-lance editorial cartoonist of the *Camden Courier Post,* illustrated the *Terry and Bunky* series of sports books for children, and built a fairly substantial free-lance business among local advertising agencies. In 1929, meanwhile, he had married Anna Mae Baldwin, by whom he had two children: Leonard Deakyne Warren, Jr., and Joyce Anna Mae Warren.

During World War II, Warren tried to enlist, but was placed in a deferred category because of his family dependents and the war-related value of his newspaper work. Accordingly, he several times weekly entertained members of the Armed Forces at nearby military camps, USO clubs, and hospitals, giving humorous "chalk talks" and performing remarkable gymnastic feats.

In 1946, the American Newspaper Guild called a strike against the *Philadelphia Record.* The work stoppage persisted over several months, during which time Warren supported his family on the proceeds of his advertising agency drawings. When, early in 1947, Mr. Stern sold his paper to the *Philadelphia Bulletin,* Warren and his colleagues lost their former regular positions.

It was a tribute to L.D.'s reputation that, at this point, he was invited to Cincinnati by Everett Boyd, managing editor of the *Cincinnati Enquirer,* to discuss the possibility of appointment as editorial cartoonist of that important paper. Previously, the Republican *Enquirer* had relied entirely for its editorial cartoons on syndicated material. Thus, if he accepted, L.D. would become the first regular editorial cartoonist of that then 107-year-old paper.

Even though the move would bring with it at least a temporary decrease in income, because of the lucrative demand for his independent work in Philadelphia, Warren decided to go to Cincinnati—where, twenty-seven years later, he retired. His first cartoon for the *Cincinnati Enquirer* appeared on July 29, 1947; it dealt with legislation for local flood-control measures. "Johnny Q" (standing for Mr. Public and based on a caricature of Warren's father) was shown using a broom, representing the necessary appropriation, and saying, "River Stay Away from My Door."

From 1951 onward, Warren's cartoons were syndicated nationally, continuing to be so disseminated until his retirement. Altogether, his work over nearly a quarter-century appeared in some two hundred newspapers, reaching more than 60,000,000 readers. His last regular cartoon as a full-time employee of the *Cincinnati Enquirer* appeared on December 1, 1973. It was a very clever and touching personal picture-story, showing his vacant rocking chair before a blank sheet on the drawing board; the caption read: "Draw Your Own Conclusion." Thereafter, he contributed occasional cartoons on local subjects to his old paper.

Anna Mae Warren did not accompany her husband to Cincinnati, and the couple were divorced in 1951. Seven years later, in 1958, he married Julianne Bussert-Baker, who herself had been divorced in 1939 and given custody of her one child, Elaine. The new Mrs. Warren, daughter of a studio-photographer, in 1941, at age twenty-five, had become general manager of a photo-finishing plant that produced 50,000 prints per day. In 1953, she became news photographer for the Democratic *Cincinnati Post,* being one of the then very few women news photographers in the United States. After sixteen years and the winning of many awards, she resigned from the paper and became a distinguished free-lance photographer, specializing in candid portraits, picture-stories, and wild life photography. The animals and birds were photographed in many of the country's major zoos and wild animal preserves, as well as in Africa and the Middle East. In 1971, she was appointed Historian of the Association of American Editorial Cartoonists.

*   *   *

In earlier pages, reference was made to the characteristics that in general have marked the work of the influential post-World War II editorial cartoonists. Because of his character, his personality, his integrity, and his approach to humanity and his profession, most of Warren's approximately 10,000 cartoons show these same characteristics. Throughout his career life, he was hardworking, and meticulous in his draftmanship. At the same time, he displayed a lively imagination and an insatiable curiosity regarding that which makes people, singly and collectively, "tick."

Distinguished by a keen sense of tolerant and kindly humor, his work consistently shows understanding of and sympathy for humanity's problems and weaknesses, as it also reflects admiration for mankind's strengths and courage. Always, L.D. is deeply respectful of man's innate dignity, simultaneously being a sharp observer and delineator of humanity's trials and errors. Ever-questioning, a prodigious reader, a deep thinker with a prescience that has enabled him to foresee an issue's or proposed solution's ramifications and consequences, he usually has picked for cartooning the things that are of fundamental and continuing importance in the life of the individual, of society, and of the world at large.

It is not possible here to list or even to summarize all L.D.'s philanthropic and patriotic activities, nor the local, national, and international awards and honors that have been accorded him. He has been more than generous over several decades with his amusing and instructive "chalk talks" to children's groups, service and social clubs, veterans' organizations, academy and college classes, and the like.

During the 1950s, he made drawing tours of the major air bases for the United States Air Force, and of Japan and Korea for the Department of Defense. In 1963, he made a drawing tour at Cape Canaveral, Florida, for the National Aeronautics and Space Administration, and in 1972 of Israel, under the sponsorship of the Press Division of the Israeli Ministry of Foreign Affairs. A number of his "safety" cartoons won awards from the National Foundation for Highways, as well as the Ohio Department of Safety. Several times the National Conference of Christians and Jews gave him its Mass Media Brotherhood Award. The patriotic Freedoms Foundation of Valley Forge, Pennsylvania, honored him with medals, prizes, and plaques more than twenty-five times between 1949 and 1974. The American Legion National Commander's Citation in Public Relations came to him in 1974.

One-man exhibitions of his work were held several times at the Art Academy of Cincinnati, the Public Library of Cincinnati and Hamilton County, the Cincinnati Art Museum, and the University of Cincinnati. He was represented in group exhibitions at the Metropolitan Museum of Art in New York (1954), the Giornate Mediche Internazionali exhibition in Verona, Italy (1963), the Pavillon International de l'Humour in Montreal (1968-1973), the National Portrait Gallery in London (1970), and the Third World Cartoon Exhibition in Skopje, Yugoslavia (1971)— where he won Honorable Mention. His works are represented in the permanent holdings of the Smithsonian Institution and of numerous universities, libraries, and museums throughout the United States. They are to be found, also, in the private collections of Presidents Harry Truman, Dwight D. Eisenhower, John F. Kennedy, Lyndon B. Johnson, Richard M. Nixon, and Gerald R. Ford.

In 1960, he was nominated for the Pulitzer Prize in editorial cartooning and in the next year he won the National Headliners Award. The National Cartoonists Society listed him as one of the "top three" American cartoonists in 1962, 1964, and 1971. During the years 1960-1964, he contributed regularly to the *Tarantel Press,* a widely-circulated anti-Communist magazine of biting humor and effective cartoons published in West Berlin.

And now we shall enjoy a selection of this genial, witty, profound, and patriotic editorial cartoonist's picture stories as accompaniment to a brief history of some of the major happenings in the world since World War II.

DRAW YOUR OWN CONCLUSION

2

COLD WAR, EUROPEAN "UNITY," AND THE UNITED NATIONS

The unusually close cooperation of the United States, Great Britain, and the Soviet Union in the fight against the Axis powers during World War II seemed to presage a postwar world of peace, upheld by this powerful trinity. France and China at times indicated unhappiness at having been left out of the Big Three conferences, but they could do little more than hope for the return of influence after the close of armed hostilities.

Allied victory, however, quickly brought disillusionment to those who had looked for continuing postwar unity. The worldwide problems facing the winners were too complex and numerous, the ideologies and self-interests too conflicting, the physical and psychological scars too deep, and the economic dislocations too severe to permit the calm and reasoning establishment of a new world. Indeed, although peace treaties were signed with Italy, Romania, Bulgaria, Hungary, and Finland in 1947, that with Japan was delayed until 1952, and an agreement with West Germany and peace with Austria were not signed until 1955.

Meanwhile, the United Nations, formed in San Francisco in 1945 to maintain peace and security while bringing about conditions of economic stability and social well-being, quickly became enmeshed in the seemingly insoluble postwar problems, and did not achieve the political authority or success that its chief Western sponsors envisioned. In reality, it was evident, by 1947, both within and outside the United Nations, that the West had come to look upon the Soviet Union as the new enemy of world freedom, and that Moscow had decided to interpret virtually all Western international proposals and actions as threats aimed at Mother Russia.

World War II thus soon was followed by a so-called Cold War between the United States and the Soviet Union. In essence, the Cold War was a long-continuing confrontation short of war, on a worldwide front, between the globe's two superpowers.

The Russian leaders took the position that Soviet industrialization and expansion were essential not alone to raise domestic living standards, but to enhance military power, itself "the price of national survival." The spread and support of Communism abroad, and the creation of a geographic "buffer" against supposed Western designs on Central and Eastern Europe, became the chief tools of Russian strategy. And so, by 1947, Romania, Poland, Hungary, Albania, Bulgaria, Yugoslavia, and Czechoslovakia had been forced within the Soviet orbit.

Winston Churchill, master of the spoken and written word, aptly summarized these developments when, in a 1946 talk at Westminster College in Missouri, he said that an "iron curtain" had "descended across the continent," thus creating a Europe wholly different from the one that the Western Allies had "fought to build up." Prophetically, too, he added that "the police governments" in Eastern Europe would not cooperate with the West to produce a peaceful Europe in future.

Hence, Great Britain and, especially, the United States gradually moved in the direction of a policy of "containment," involving the use of "counterforce" to Moscow's policy of constantly shifting geographical and political thrusts "to keep the pot boiling." Simultaneously, the Soviet Union insisted on keeping Germany divided* and eventually, in 1955, forged among its satellite states the Warsaw Treaty Organization. This was called a counterweight to the North Atlantic Treaty Organization (NATO), created in 1949, and joined by West Germany in 1955. Originally formed mainly to prevent possible renewed aggression by a revived Germany, NATO soon became a Western alliance aimed at protecting its members against attack from Soviet-dominated Eastern Europe.

For a decade or so after World War II, the possession of atomic-weapons superiority by the United States provided a measure of security for the democracies. But then, the launching of a half-ton satellite (Sputnik I) into orbit by the Soviet Union in 1957 marked the beginning of what came to be called not a balance of power, but a "rocket-rattling balance of terror."

Meanwhile, Moscow successfully had pursued a policy of keeping the West, and especially the United States, on tenterhooks over outbreaks at widely separated trouble spots beyond Europe. At little cost to herself, Russia's activities led to the expenditure of vast American economic resources and considerable loss of life through the precipitation of crises

---

*In 1948-1949, the Soviet Union blockaded Berlin by cutting off ground access across the Soviet Occupation Zone, a blockade that was broken by a remarkable "air lift" of persons and goods from the West. And in 1961, to halt the large outflow of Germans from East Germany to West Germany, a guarded wall of barbed wire and concrete was erected by the Communists between East and West Berlin.

such as the Korean War (1950-1953), the Cuban missiles dispute (1962), and the struggle in Vietnam (1956-1973).*

Only in the 1970s did General Secretary of the Communist Party Leonid I. Brezhnev react with apparent favor to the proposal of President Richard M. Nixon for détente. Fragile as this "new" relation appeared, it did inspire some in the West to hope for an extended prolongation of peace. Others, however, were less optimistic. They remembered the traditional response of both Tsarist and Soviet rulers whenever their expansionist plans appeared checked, namely, to retreat when necessary, and then to launch the struggle anew when preoccupation otherwise of Western Europe and Eastern Asia made circumstances once again look propitious for Russian imperialism.

Meanwhile, the events and results of World War II and the Cold War gave stimulus to a major and continuing movement for the establishment of some sort of unity among the states of Western and Central Europe. Gradually, more and more European statesmen recognized that their individual countries no longer were strong and rich enough to play leading roles in world affairs.

In an age of atomic power and space travel, they were weakened by the loss of empire and found it increasingly difficult individually to afford the financial burden of maintaining scientific and technological parity with the superpowers centered in Washington and Moscow. The unhindered Russian invasion of Czechoslovakia, in 1968, made it yet clearer, if that were necessary, that the former Great Powers were helpless without unity. Any hope of matching in strength the United States and the U.S.S.R. would require a "Third Force," comprising a like-acting population of several hundred millions, with a "gross national product" (GNP) approaching a trillion dollars.

Already in 1947, Secretary of State George C. Mashall, with the approval of President Truman, announced a European Recovery Program (ERP). This Marshall Plan was intended, through large-scale American economic aid over a period of years, to help Europe help itself, and thus also lessen the danger of economic disaster and political turmoil on the continent. Russia brusquely denounced the Plan as an imperialistic attempt to establish United States dominance over Europe. But for the European states west of the Iron Curtain, it provided opportunity for some sort of cooperative action.

In 1948, then, there came into being an Organization for European Economic Cooperation (OEEC), which, late in 1960, was re-formed as

---

*Throughout the thirty years immediately following World War II, an age-old Sino-Russian enmity kept flaring, in vituperation and in military clashes, along the 4500-mile joint border. The situation became especially worrisome after mainland China, too, became an atomic power, in the early 1970s.

the Organization for Economic Cooperation and Development (OECD). Made up, in 1973, of twenty-three states, including the United States, Japan, Canada, and Australia, its purposes were to maximize the members' economic growth, assist the developing countries, contribute to the orderly expansion of world trade, and propose ways to strengthen the international monetary system. Some improvement did occur in all these spheres, but, quite early, it was clear that additional, sometimes parallel, organizations were needed. Yet, inevitably, the proliferation of international agencies with related purposes led to overlapping responsibilities and a frustrating weakening of several of the groups.

As the OEEC was founded on an economic base, so, in 1949, the Council of Europe was established to seek a rational basis for Europe's future political relations. There were seventeen members in 1973, with a headquarters building in Strasbourg. Without significant authority, and in the absence among the states of a "common political will," this council spent most of its time in talk and conferences. Its prime achievement, perhaps, was the creation of a European Commission on Human Rights; but this body, too, could do little beyond "examining" and publicizing alleged violations by member countries. In recent years, the council has encouraged East European participation in its deliberations.

The Treaty of Paris (1951) gave life, in 1952, to an effective European Coal and Steel Community (ECSC) among the six leading continental producers, namely, Belgium, France, Italy, Luxembourg, the Netherlands, and West Germany. With headquarters in Luxembourg, its purposes were to "fuse" markets by removing barriers to the coal and steel trade, improve living standards, and point toward the eventual economic and political unity of Europe. The High Authority of the ECSC was in effect a supranational body, whose members were forbidden to receive instructions from their national governments; it was endowed with full regulatory power over the production, distribution, and pricing of coal and steel among the constituent nations. A special Court of Justice was set up to adjudicate disputes and to judge and punish policy violations.

Rome was the signing site of a 1957 treaty that brought into being, in 1958, a European Atomic Energy Community (EURATOM) to channel unified nuclear research into peaceful avenues. It was composed of the same six members as the ECSC, namely, Benelux (Belgium, the Netherlands, and Luxembourg), France, Italy, and West Germany. In the ensuing years, it established four joint nuclear research centers, strove to coordinate national research programs, gave guidance as well as technical and financial aid to private atomic projects, and developed safeguards for the handling and distribution of fissionable material.

The 1968 Treaty on the Non-Proliferation of Nuclear Weapons, open for signature to all countries, forecast some inspection authority for

EURATOM, but the major nuclear powers, including some EURATOM members, had not ratified the document by 1974. Meanwhile, too, the development and spread to many countries, for military and prestige reasons, of national research programs and production potential hampered the EURATOM by bringing continuing cuts in contributions to its budget.

On the same day, in 1957, on which EURATOM was created in Rome, another agreement among the same six powers established, effective in 1958, the European Economic Community (EEC), popularly called the Common Market (CM). The long-range objectives of this most far-reaching of the steps toward European unity were defined as bringing the respective populations more closely together, while simultaneously raising their living standards. It was implied that the economic unity pursued by this Brussels-headquartered Community eventually would be followed by monetary and political union—with a target date for total integration later, optimistically, set at 1980.

Before considering the CM, let us note that the Treaty of Brussels (1965), effective in the summer of 1967, combined the ECSC, EURATOM, and the EEC into a collective organization known as the European Communities (EC). The overall structure included, in 1974, the policy-setting Council of Ministers (usually foreign ministers) directly representing the member governments; an administrative arm in Brussels, called the Commission and composed of 13 international civil servants known as Commissioners; an Assembly or European Parliament of 198 representatives, meeting in Luxembourg and concerned chiefly with discussion and the focusing of public opinion; and a Court of Justice to determine violations of the EC treaties and policy, and to assess fines for noncompliance by businesses and other economic units. As of January 1, 1973, the six members of the European Communities were joined by Denmark, Great Britain, and Ireland, thus converting the "Inner Six" into the "Community of Nine."

The basic assignment of the European Economic Community was the development of a customs union, with no tariffs among the members, and a uniform tariff against all nonmembers. In agriculture, where the hasty elimination of tariffs and such other trade barriers as quotas would have created general chaos and hardship for the individual farmers, and in interstate transportation, it was agreed to follow a slower schedule of tariff elimination than in the case of manufactured goods. The existing governmental trading monopolies, such as those in tobacco, also were to be done away with over a period of years.

To some observers, it appeared that the chief weakness of the CM was the rapid schedule adopted for European integration. In actuality, the "harmonization" process was agonizingly slow in the eyes of the Commissioners in Brussels, but unrealistically fast in the view of many government officials, businessmen, and members of the general public.

The specific obstacles to implementation of the standardization program were numerous. They included conflicts between short-term and long-range national and individual interests; domestic political considerations and ambitions, as demonstrated most clearly during the period of oil shortages; and differing philosophies of life, such as France's strong belief that Great Britain really "was not at all European." The members were at uneven stages of economic development, and the former colonial powers were eager to continue special economic arrangements with their erstwhile dependencies. Some of the proposed international guidelines were inapplicable to particular national situations. And, except among some of the youth, there was only a slow movement away from existing diverse and emotional national spirits toward a European spirit.

Moreover, the gradual disappearance of tariffs, state monopolies, and variances in standards of product size, composition, and performance was accompanied by a proliferation of ingenious nontariff barriers or so-called technical obstacles to trade. Hundreds of such obstacles were hidden in fussy health regulations, supposedly necessary social legislation, tricky tax structures, arbitrary quota systems, overly technical medical restrictions, "service charges" at frontier posts, specified advantages to domestic bidders on public contracts, and the like. Some of these represented outright evasion; but, in many cases, the attempt to prescribe identical procedural standards for nine different countries was unnecessary, unreasonable, or even nonsensical.

Nonetheless, the European Communities had an estimated (1974) total population of 253,000,000, compared to 210,000,000 for the United States. And this in an area of 590,000 square miles, or less than one-sixth that of the 3,600,000 square miles that makes up the United States. The overall economic status of each member population *was* improved by such integration as had been achieved, and, by 1973, the EC had a gross national product of $800,000,000,000,000 (compared to $1,200,000,000,000 for the United States), and accounted for 40 percent of the world's trade.

During these years of hesitant European integration, the United Nations, with headquarters in New York, was finding it difficult to meet the four basic goals assigned to it by its charter of 1945. The stated purposes were to maintain peace, develop friendly international relations, foster worldwide cooperation in nonpolitical matters, and promote universal respect for human dignity and freedom. The organization's members, numbering 51 in 1945 and 138 at the end of 1974, had one vote each in the General Assembly. The Security Council originally had five permanent and six nonpermanent members; in 1966, the number of nonpermanent members rose to ten. Each of the permanent members—China, France, the U.S.S.R., the United Kingdom, and the United States—was given veto power over any substantive decision. All states in the

United Nations agreed to "recognize" the sovereign equality of every country, regardless of size, and to resolve their international disputes without force.

The degree of success attainable to the United Nations obviously depended on the willingness of the constituents to live up to their obligations. At the start, particularly in the Security Council, this responsibility lay heaviest on the Great Powers. From about 1965, especially in the General Assembly, it rested equally heavily on such cooperating groups of smaller states as the Latin-American bloc and the Afro-Asian bloc. In the first two decades of the United Nations' existence, a number of relatively minor though potentially dangerous international disagreements were guided to peaceable outcome. But where major-power interests were affected, and in the matter of disarmament, the record was less gratifying.

For some twenty-five years, the Soviet Union dramatized the ability of a large state to obstruct the efforts of a majority in the society. The Russians used liberally, indeed, almost monopolistically, their absolute veto authority in the Security Council.* Moscow also frequently persuaded its satellites in the General Assembly to join in wholesale vote abstentions, and itself resorted to insult and falsification as regular tools of procedure. In 1960, Nikita Khrushchev set a new standard of debasement by pounding one of his shoes on a desk while an opponent was trying to speak.

The strength of the Afro-Asian bloc became pronounced from 1971, in which year Nationalist China was deprived of its membership and Security Council seat in favor of Communist China. In 1973, the General Assembly, while not expelling the Union of South Africa, rejected the credentials of its delegation. And in 1974, the General Assembly gave a voice and the privileges usually reserved for the heads of member states to Yassir Arafat, leader of the (Arab) Palestine Liberation Organization. Meanwhile, these and other similar unrestrained acts and postures, not foreseen in 1945, brought to a low level the moral authority of the UN and its hoped-for status as a spokesman for reasonable and peaceable world opinion.

On the other hand, the picture was brighter where the activities of UN agencies in the nonpolitical sphere were concerned, namely, in the areas of economic, cultural, and humanitarian improvement. Effective technical assistance was rendered to developing nations. Agricultural productivity was raised in many parts of the world. The lot of children was bettered in a number of countries, disease was fought successfully on many fronts, and life was made easier for millions through the efforts of devoted UN civil servants.

---

*By March, 1974, Russia had posted 107 vetoes out of a total of 127. The United States used its veto power for the first time in 1972.

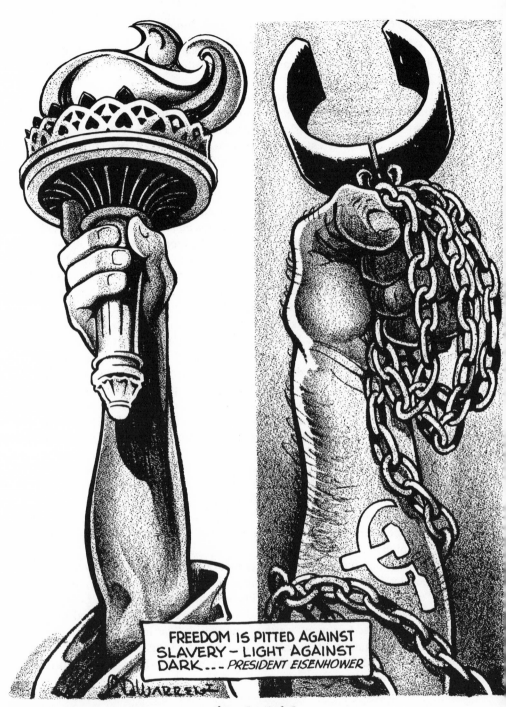

FREEDOM IS PITTED AGAINST
SLAVERY — LIGHT AGAINST
DARK... *PRESIDENT EISENHOWER*

WITH FIRMNESS IN THE RIGHT

THE GHOST WALKS

BUT – A COMMUNIST IS A COMMUNIST IS A COMMUNIST

LIP SERVICE

JANUS—LEFT AND RIGHT   —By L. D. Warren

MARTIAL PLAN TO SLAVE EUROPE   MARSHALL PLAN TO SAVE EUROPE

"ALL YOUR SPINACH, FIRST!"

"I GET A LIFT OUT OF MINE!"

TIME TO GET OUT THE LONGIES

JUST IN CASE

'MAY I SUGGEST ALL PASSENGERS IN THE REAR SEAT GET OUT AND PUSH!'

'NOTHING TRIVIAL, I HOPE!'

BERLIN BLOCKADE

WHEN THE BOUGH BREAKS-THE CRADLE WILL FALL

'AAW SHADDUP — IT'S JUST THE SAME OLD WESTERN PLOT!'

"LET'S JUST SHAKE HANDS!"

'NOTHING LIKE A COZY FIRESIDE FOR AN AGREEABLE CHAT!'

THIS CHEEK TURNING CAN GET MONOTONOUS

GIVE MANKIND ENOUGH ROPE....

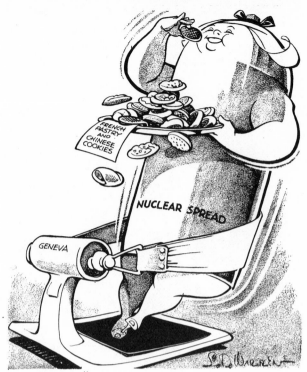

'IT TICKLES ME!'

'I'D BETTER TAKE A SECOND LOOK AT THAT LOCK!'

THAT'S WHAT MAKES PARIS, PAREE

'HEY_DO EITHER OF YOU FELLOWS KNOW A MADEMOISELLE MARIANNE?'

'IT'S NOT VERY COMFORTABLE, IS IT?'

'WHAT DO YOU THINK OF THESE MODERN METHODS?'

'BE PATIENT, I'M SURE I'LL FIND IT HERE SOMEWHERE!'

'MAYBE HE WANTS TO COME IN, CHARLES!'

DARK THE NIGHT AND WILD THE STORM

THE CRUCIBLE AND THE MOLD

'ALLAH!'

'HERE – IT TAKES ALL THE RUNNING YOU CAN DO, TO KEEP IN THE SAME PLACE, IF YOU WANT TO GET SOMEWHERE ELSE, YOU MUST RUN TWICE AS FAST AS THAT!'

'TOO BAD - POOR FELLOW - SHOULD HAVE BEEN MORE ALERT'

'BEFORE YOU LEAVE - A FREE SOUVENIR FOR CHARTER MEMBERS!'

TRYING TO STEAL THE SHOW BETWEEN ACTS

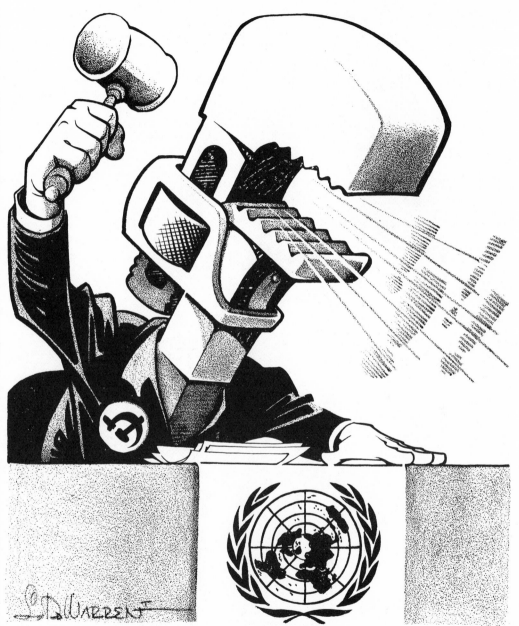

'THIS MEETING WILL NOW COME TO DISORDER!'

TOWER OF BABEL

"SHE LOVES ME!"

"HOLD YOUR BREATH WHILE WE TAKE A VOTE!"

"HOW MANY TIMES MUST I TELL YOU TO KEEP OUT OF THERE?"

'IT'S EASY— JUST WALK IN AND SAY BOO!'

LEANING TOWER OF NEW YORK

'WAKE UP! IT'S TIME FOR A CHANGE! AND I'M TIRED OF GETTING SOAKED!'

'SORRY! THAT'S YOUR DEPARTMENT—I'M STEERING!'

'YOU MAY FORCE ME TO REMOVE YOUR HAND — HELP ME UP!'

'MAYBE FOR A VISIT, BUT I'D HATE TO LIVE THERE!'

3

THE UNITED KINGDOM

The parliamentary coalition that governed Great Britain during World War II fell apart after victory. In July, 1945, the voters repudiated Sir Winston Churchill and gave the Labor party a majority in the House of Commons. Clement R. Attlee, formerly a lecturer at the London School of Economics, became prime minister. The new government, influenced strongly by labor union leaders, contemplated transformation of the kingdom into a "Socialist Commonwealth." It, and later Labor governments, in effect, adopted as pragmatic the view of John M. Keynes that "what we can do, we can afford."

The first steps were not startling. Legislation was enacted to provide housing for some 300,000 families whose dwelling places had been rendered uninhabitable by bombing. Public educational opportunities were expanded on all levels from primary grades through university. Insurance systems were set up to give financial help in the event of unemployment, sickness, and the death of a family wage-earner, and to assist with maternity costs.

Then, however, a National Health Service was established to provide, originally without any charge and later with some slight payment, medical, dental, optical, and hospital services as well as medication and medical appliances to every person living in the kingdom. Physicians in general became civil servants and were assigned to specific health stations; often a physician had to serve as many as 3000 patients.

Nationalization of industry proceeded apace. The overseas wireless services and the Bank of England were nationalized in 1946; coal mining and much of transport were taken over in 1947; electrical and gas services had their turn in 1948, and iron and steel production in 1949. Previous owners were compensated and government corporations were created to operate the businesses. Usually the cost of operation was much higher than had been the case under private ownership.

In the regular election of 1950, Labor held on to a small majority. It was apparent, however, that the pressures and crises attending the rapid changes, which came so soon after the trauma of the war, were somewhat less than popular. The appearance of an adverse trade balance, the new costs resulting from Britain's support of United Nations forces in Korea, and the prospect of a tremendous increase in the next budget caused so much discontent that Attlee called another election in 1951. This time the Conservatives and their allies won a majority and Churchill returned as prime minister. A few months after the election, King George VI died and was succeeded by his daughter, Queen Elizabeth II.

While continuing to provide more housing and expand social insurance plans, the new government denationalized some industries, such as iron and steel, and found ways to improve the economy. In 1955, the eighty-year-old Churchill passed the leadership to Sir Anthony Eden, a highly respected diplomat. His Conservative party won another major parliamentary election victory in the same year. But the awkward Anglo-French-Israeli invasion of Egypt in 1956, over control of the Suez Canal, with a resultant break in Anglo-American cooperation, brought much criticism of Eden. Increasing unemployment coupled with renewed inflation added to the prime minister's burden, and he soon resigned on advice of his physicians. In 1957, Conservative and parliamentary leadership went to Harold Macmillan.

The latter healed the Anglo-American breach and improved the country's financial position. Exports increased, employment went up, and property ownership became more widely distributed. Manufacturing flourished, compact British automobiles sold well abroad, and company earnings and stock prices rose gratifyingly.

On the negative side, new economic and social problems appeared with a rapidly growing native population and an unprecedented influx of West Indians, Asian Indians, Pakistani, and Africans. A morals scandal involving the war minister added to the growing public discontent. Hence, although the Conservatives won another parliamentary election victory in 1959, they lost to the Laborites by a narrow margin toward the end of 1964. This margin was boosted to a comfortable Labor majority in the special election of 1966.

The Labor leader, Harold Wilson, resorted to stern measures involving both domestic and foreign policies. Corporate mergers were restricted severely, numerous defense projects were dropped, the number of armed forces overseas was slashed, taxes were raised, and the pound sterling was devalued. Meanawhile, a number of Commonwealth members either broke away entirely from or effectively loosened their ties to Great Britain. Moreover, certain elements in the Republic of Ireland resorted to violence in a renewed effort to absorb Northern Ireland.

All this led to a growing sentiment for British membership in the European Communities, particularly the Economic Community or Common Market. But every approach by London was vetoed by the France of President Charles de Gaulle, on the ground that the kingdom was too closely linked with the United States to enable her to pursue a "European" policy. The elections of 1970 not unexpectedly returned the Conservatives to power, under Prime Minister Edward Heath.

The Heath government obviously had to wrestle with the same problems that had made life difficult for its predecessor. A rapid rate of inflation and a variety of labor grievances led to damaging work stoppages in 1972. The result was reduced production, a further loss in overseas trade, and a drop in the value of the pound sterling. When labor and management failed to agree on a voluntary price-control program, Parliament approved a mandatory standstill or "freeze" on prices, wages, dividends, and rents, effective at the end of November, 1972.

Meanwhile, there was a worsening situation in Northern Ireland and a sudden influx of immigrants from Africa. Against the wishes of the Dublin government in the Republic of Ireland, members of the illegal Irish Republican Army perpetrated almost daily outrages and murders in (largely Protestant) Northern Ireland, especially in the Belfast area. There were religious as well as economic and political overtones to the crisis, which no one seemed able to settle. In March, 1972, London suspended the separate Northern Ireland Parliament and prime minister; thereafter the area was administered by a secretary of state in London. An agreement by the Protestant majority in 1973 to share power with the Catholic minority did little to lessen the murders and bombings.

Meanwhile, when President Idi Amin Dada of Uganda, in the fall of 1972, ordered some 54,000 Asian Indians who held British passports to leave the country within ninety days, about 28,000 of them were given emergency air transportation to Great Britain. The coming of this wave of refugees aggravated not merely economic and housing problems, but added fuel to a simmering racial confrontation.

On January 1, 1973, the United Kingdom at last became a member of the Common Market. This, the government hoped, would result in an economic upturn and a lessening of the people's restlessness. But before time for a fair trial had elapsed, there came an economy-crippling coal strike, followed soon by a shortage of imported oil as a result of an embargo, and then unprecedented price increases, imposed by the Arabic oil-producing countries as a ploy to force a strong Western stand against Israel. The London government in desperation, and perhaps to gain sympathy from the public, ordained a three-day work week.

Hoping for a major public endorsement of his policies, Heath arranged for parliamentary elections in February, 1974. Neither the Conservatives nor the Laborites won a majority, but the latter were supported by enough of the minor party members, especially the Liberals, to form a government. Harold Wilson thereupon became prime minister. He conceded nearly every one of the striking miners' demands, thus promptly worsening the rate of inflation, announced an intention to lead the country to Socialism, and promised a referendum on continuing Common Market membership in 1975.

--- AND TEARS

CAREFUL DOC—HE'S HUNGRY —By L. D. Warren

"STOP! YOU KNOW WHAT HAPPENED BEFORE!"

BEGINNING THE LONG HAUL

65

'THIS WAS THEIR FINEST HOUR'

'YES, NOW! WHILE THEY'RE STILL APPLAUDING!'

'FORSOOTH, LITTLE JOHNSON! WHAT SHALL WE DOEST AFTER WE TAKETH FROM THE LAST INDUSTRIOUS ONE?'

'WOULDN'T YOU SAY MY TAIL OF WOE PRESENTS A KNOTTY PROBLEM, MR. HEATH?'

TIGHT LITTLE ISLE

'CLOSE THAT WINDOW, EDWARD! DO YOU WANT ME TO CATCH PNEUMONIA?'

'HOW DO YOU KNOW YOU CAN'T DO IT WITHOUT TRYING?'

'WASSA IDEA SPENDIN' OUR MONEY ON GROCERIES?'

'AD LEAST, WE HAB SOMDING IN COMMON – SHALL WE BLAME MR. KENNEDY?'

LAST FOOTING IN ARABIA

72

SOS

'WHAT'S A MOTHER TO DO?'

4

THE FOURTH AND FIFTH FRENCH REPUBLICS

Postwar France experienced a spirit of divisiveness that boded ill for the future. Reprisals against former Nazi collaborators, Communist take-overs in some parts of the country, the effects of wartime destruction; unemployment; the plight of returning prisoners of war and laborers who had been forced to work in Germany; and disagreements over a new form of government, all made the outlook bleak. Gradually, however, more and more Frenchmen looked to General Charles de Gaulle to set up a government strong enough to bring recovery and stability.

In October, 1945, a provisional government, headed by de Gaulle and representing several resistance groups, ordered a referendum, with women voting for the first time. The voters in effect rejected a revived Third Republic by electing a Constituent Assembly to draft a constitution. De Gaulle, now president of the provisional government, urged a governing system that would make the executive dominant over the legislature. Finding strong resistance to his opinion, the somewhat imperious de Gaulle resigned in January, 1946.

The assembly thereupon drew up a Leftist-oriented document, making a figurehead of the president. When this draft was voted down, the assembly prepared another one, this time somewhat enlarging the executive's authority. The second document was approved in another referendum, and the Fourth Republic came into being toward the close of 1946. The Socialist, Vincent Auriol, became president.

During the period 1946-1951, eight ministries rose and fell. None of them was able to halt inflation, strikes, and unrest. When the United States offered economic aid through the Marshall Plan in 1947, the French Communists openly fomented strikes and agitated for acceptance of Soviet rather than American aid. These and other activities of the Reds served largely to move public sentiment to the Right, and the election of 1951 brought to power a coalition made up of the pro-Gaullist *Movement Républicain Populaire* (MRP), the Socialists, and the Radicals (who were to the Right of the Socialists). For a number of years, Premier Jean Monnet gave effective leadership to the Fourth Republic.

His government voted heavy investment in railways, mines, and hydroelectric plants. Production of steel, automobiles, farm equipment, and concrete materials was stimulated. In all this, the Marshall Plan (1947) was of immeasurable help. During the early 1950s, fifteen of France's twenty leading industries reached their greatest productivity in peacetime history. Population simultaneously rose rapidly, while the economic gap between rich and poor shrank noticeably. Taxes, of course, increased steadily.

Agricultural prosperity, however, despite the widespread introduction of farm machinery, lagged behind industrial progress. As a consequence, and because of the seeming attractions of urban life, about one-fourth of the peasantry left the land during the first postwar decade. France's founding membership (1957) in the European Economic Community or Common Market was especially helpful to much of agriculture and probably staved off a more serious agrarian decline. Over all, the groups that benefitted least from the reviving economy were the small shopkeepers, unskilled workers, and peasants with minimal holdings.

Foreign affairs, meanwhile, had been kept on a fairly even keel, and France's international eminence had been restored, under the alternating Foreign Office leadership of Georges Bidault and Robert Schuman. Imbued with a "European" spirit, they weaned France from isolation to membership in several associations, including the Council of Europe and NATO in 1949, and then the Common Market. Fear of renewed European dominance by a reviving Germany, however, continued to haunt many Frenchmen. And the Fourth Republic lost prestige, money, and the blood of many of its finest youth in unsuccessful efforts to retain control of overseas territories, notably in North Africa and Southeast Asia.

In Asia, the French withdrew from their Indochinese empire in 1954. The action followed a disastrous French defeat at Dien Bien Phu and the signing of the Geneva Protocols. Two years later, France cut her political ties to Morocco and Tunisia in North Africa. But the situation in respect of Algeria, where lived more than a million Frenchmen, was more complicated.

A campaign for independence launched by Algerian Nationalists resulted in the commitment to the area of some 350,000 French troops by 1956. For years, no premier dared to advocate withdrawal because of the objection of the numerous *colons* or French settlers (some of whose families had lived in Algeria for generations) and the opposition of the military, which was loath to lose all its imperial influence. And actually, when Premier Pierre Pflimlin, in 1958, did plan to propose withdrawal to his Cabinet, extremists in Algeria resorted to violence and the government feared an extension of the turmoil to the mother country. At this juncture, de Gaulle announced his willingness to save France, if he were called upon to do so as premier.

President René Coty issued such a call and agreed to de Gaulle's conditions that he be given decree power for six months, at the end of which period he would submit a new constitution to referendum. In due time, a new draft was presented to the electorate which responded favorably by a vote of four to one. Thenceforth, legislative power was to be exercised by the premier rather than the assembly, and the indirectly elected president was authorized to nominate the prime minister. De Gaulle now promptly was chosen president. He took office in January, 1959. Thus ended the Fourth Republic and was born the Fifth Republic.

Among the first external acts of the new government was the grant to fifteen French territories in West and Equatorial Africa and to Madagascar of a choice between self-government within a French community or independence Eventually, all chose separatism, although several did keep close cultural and even economic ties to France. In the fall of 1959, de Gaulle offered self-determination to Algeria.

This angered the *colons* and the army, for they had expected de Gaulle, as a military man, to stand for continuing French hegemony. Consequently, after a plebiscite in France in 1961 upheld the president's offer, some *colons* and a portion of the armed forces seized Algiers and other cities in Algeria. Rumor had it that the so-called Secret Army Organization (OAS) would march on Paris itself. De Gaulle thereupon, over national television, called on all loyal Frenchmen for support against the conspiracy. Widespread pro-de Gaulle demonstrations followed, and loyal troops were sent to restore order in Algeria. Fighting continued until the reaching of a ceasefire agreement in March, 1962. Referenda in both France and Algeria endorsed the agreement, and, in July, Algeria became independent. Nearly a million *colons* left their homes to take up a new life in France.*

During the 1960s, de Gaulle appointed loyal but generally colorless persons to high position, all the while arrogating more and more power to himself. The material well-being of the populace appeared for a time to make it relatively indifferent to the government's structure, although the Socialists vigorously attacked what they labeled an "elective monarchy." But the popular attitude began to change after 1965, and in the elections of 1967 de Gaulle's parliamentary majority became slim.

In foreign relations, meanwhile, de Gaulle tried to establish for France

---

*Meanwhile, in 1962 also, another referendum accepted de Gaulle's proposal for a constitutional amendment providing for direct election of the president.

a position as the "Third Force" between the United States and the U.S.S.R. Since he looked upon the United Kingdom as being much under American influence, he also adopted a strong stand against the British. Thus, as had been indicated, he exercised the veto power from 1963 onward to keep Great Britain out of the Common Market. He made of France a nuclear power and then gradually withdrew French forces from NATO. In 1967, he forced NATO headquarters out of France and was content to see it move to Brussels. Simultaneously, de Gaulle made overtures to the Communist world, negotiating treaties with Moscow and recognizing Communist China in 1964. Only after the Russian invasion of Czechoslovakia did he indicate that it might be necessary to reevaluate the advantages of NATO to France.

In 1968, France began to experience student demonstrations similar to those in other countries—a situation made worse by the formation of a temporary alliance of the youth with industrial workers, who took over some of the factories. Apparently the real though somewhat nebulous basis for the unrest was not so much economic difficulty as a feeling that the government was excessively paternalistic and authoritarian and therefore unresponsive to the deeper needs of the citizenry.

De Gaulle eventually conceded the desirability of change, particularly in the outworn educational structure and in working conditions, especially among the blue-collar group. Typically, he then requested sweeping power to restructure France's future, and again threatened to resign if his proposal was rejected in a referendum. The reaction among the dissidents was a renewal of disorder and strikes on a scale so large as to arouse among the general population a fear of anarchy. In place of a referendum, then, new elections were held in June, 1968, and the Gaullists won a resounding victory.

Not content with this triumph, *Le Grand Charles* ordered a referendum in 1969 on a series of recommendations to weaken the Senate and further strengthen the presidency. This time, the general lost—and resigned. (He died in 1970 and, at his direction, was buried in the small town of his birth.) A special election now gave the presidency to Georges Pompidou, who had served as premier under de Gaulle.

Pompidou generally followed de Gaulle's policies, except that he favored devaluing the franc—a step that he thought would improve foreign trade. In order to permit implementation of the educational and social reforms that the Gaullist Parliament had enacted in 1968, Pompidou found it necessary to slacken the military program and postpone for a year, to 1970, some planned Pacific atomic tests. Abroad, he strove to rebuild French influence in Africa and the Middle East and to extend it among the Communist bloc countries. A referendum in 1972 endorsed his recommendation to vote in favor of Common Market membership for several countries, including Great Britain.

The president's chief problem seemed to be a growing divergence in interpretation among Gaullists as to what really constituted "Gaullism," while at the same time the numerous Leftist groups were drawing together more closely. In the parliamentary elections of 1973, however, the Gaullist-oriented elements still won the victory. And when Pompidou died of cancer in March, 1974, the people chose as his successor his former minister for finance and economic affairs, Valéry Giscard d'Estaing. This third president of the Fifth Republic, was far less rigid in both manner and thought than were his two predecessors.

'WHY DO YOU THINK I MARRIED HIM?'

'MAY I LOOK NOW?'

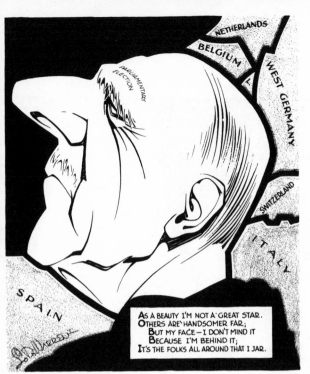

NETHERLANDS

BELGIUM

WEST GERMANY

SWITZERLAND

ITALY

SPAIN

PARLIAMENTARY ELECTION

As A BEAUTY I'M NOT A GREAT STAR.
OTHERS ARE HANDSOMER FAR;
  BUT MY FACE — I DON'T MIND IT
  BECAUSE I'M BEHIND IT;
IT'S THE FOLKS ALL AROUND THAT I JAR.

THE FACE IS FAMILIAR

DOMESTIC RELATIONS

'NON-SUPPORT, YOUR HONOR!'

'REGARDEZ, MA MERE! NO CAVITIES!'

LONG HARD PULL

83

'I'D SAY HE'S RATHER SHORT ON TEAM WORK — WOULDN'T YOU?'

'IF THIS DOESN'T MAKE ME THE GREATEST, I'LL EAT MY HELMET!'

84

'I GUESS HE WANTS TO BE SURE HE'S SAFE ON FIRST!'

'WHAT'S IN A NAME? THAT WHICH WE CALL A ROSE BY ANY OTHER NAME WOULD SMELL AS SWEET.'

'BUT I DON'T WANT TO GO OUT AND PLAY LIKE THE OTHER KIDS!'

'WHAT'S THE MATTER, CHARLES? YOU LOOK LIKE YOU'VE SEEN A GHOST!

'WHAT WILL YOU PAY ME IF I DON'T WORK FOR EITHER?'

'JE SUIS POOPED! WHAT'S FOR DINNER, MARIANNE?'

'HEADS I WIN — TAILS YOU LOSE!'

SAVED BY LA BELLE!

'TCH! TCH! JUST LOOK OLD CHARLIE MAKING A FOOL OF HIMSELF!'

'THEY LOVED ME IN MONTREAL!'

BIG FOUR REUNION

5

GERMANY: WEST IS WEST
AND EAST IS EAST

Toward the close of World War II, Russia, without seeking prior agreement from its allies, took over the northern half of East Prussia. Simultaneously taking also a large slice of Eastern Poland, Moscow blithely compensated Warsaw by placing under "Polish Administration" all German territory east of an arbitrary line formed by the Oder-Neisse rivers.

Then, at the Potsdam Conference (July-August, 1945), Russia insisted successfully that the remainder of Germany be divided into Zones of Occupation. The division resulted in a Soviet zone to the East, and United States, British, and French zones to the West. The four zones were to be administered by respective zone commanders under the supervision of the Allied Control Council. Berlin similarly was divided into four Occupation sectors and placed under the control of the Inter-Allied Commission. Inasmuch as Berlin was wholly within the Soviet zone, the Western allies were guaranteed ground, canal, and air access to the old capital. (Austria and Vienna, respectively, likewise were divided into occupation zones and sectors.)

The Big Four at Potsdam agreed, further, to "denazify" and demilitarize Germany, to try "war criminals," and to divest Germany of future war-making potential. The Soviets, in vigorously pursuing this last goal, confiscated and removed to Russia virtually all industrial equipment found in the Soviet zone and much that was in the Western occupation zones. An agreement that all Germany would be treated "as a single economic unit" was disregarded by Moscow from the very beginning. As the Cold War developed, the Western allies ceased dismantling German factories and encouraged the growth of a self-supporting economy in West Germany. Moscow, meanwhile, continued to prevent the negotiation of a German peace treaty—in 1968 going so far as to imply that reunification and peace could come about only after West Germany, too, had become a "socialist" state.

In the Western zones, the occupiers soon permitted the Germans to assume responsibility for many governmental functions and allowed the revival of political parties. The Communist party was reorganized rapidly and soon became the fourth largest in each of the Western zones. When these zones were united in 1949 as the Federal Republic of Germany, the Communists openly followed the Moscow "line." Thereupon, however, they quickly lost their voter appeal and, in 1956, the party was outlawed as being unconstitutional.

The strongest West German party was the Christian Democratic Union (CDU). It was formed through a coalition of several pre-Hitler elements, the largest among which was the Catholic Center party. The CDU basically was a religiously oriented, patriotic, middle-class group, headed by Dr. Konrad Adenauer, sometime mayor of Cologne and affectionately known as *Der Alte*. Becoming Chancellor in 1949 at age seventy-three, he retained office until his resignation in 1963. The Social Democrats (SPD) were next in strength, with a platform that was moderately socialistic and anticlerical, strongly social-welfare oriented, and singularly nationalistic. Third among the major groupings was the Free Democratic party (FDP), which stood to the right of the CDU, was strongly nationalistic, and heavily stressed the importance of free enterprise.

Meanwhile, in 1948, the Western powers informed Moscow that its uncooperativeness in the drafting of a German peace treaty forced them to proceed with the establishment of a new state, pending the reunion of West and East Germany. In 1949, the West Germans adopted a democratic "Basic Law" to serve as constitution until reunification. This document was approved by the Western Allies, who then formally recognized the Federal Republic of Germany, with its capital at Bonn. Shortly thereafter, the Russians permitted the East German Communists to establish the German Democratic Republic, with its capital in East Berlin.

In 1953, the Western Allies went further and agreed to replace the occupation statute with a convention that returned virtual sovereignty to West Germany, but permitted the stationing of Allied troops on German soil as a deterrent to possible Russian aggression. Two years later, Germany became a member of NATO. As long as Adenauer was chancellor, moreover, a firm line was held regarding the goal of reunification and a refusal to recognize Poland's hegemony over the former German lands east of the Oder-Neisse Line.

As chancellor, heading a moderate coalition, Adenauer strove in domestic affairs to encourage profit-making combined with a recognition by employers of their responsibility for the civic and social welfare of the community. In foreign relations, he aimed at rebuilding the armed forces so that Germany could assist the Western Allies in the defense of Europe, elimination of the traditional Franco-German hostility, friendship with the United States, reunification with East Germany, and the economic integration of Europe. He succeeded in reaching all these objectives save reunification.

Adenauer's ability to attract voter support eventually led the Socialists to move away from doctrinaire Marxism. After Willy Brandt in 1952 became leader of the Social Democrats, the party platform soft-pedalled its utopian dreams and emphasized immediate social and political legislation that might be expected to appeal to the masses. In 1969, they gained the opportunity for leadership.

Two CDU successors to Adenauer were unable to exploit further the republic's economic successes. Nor, despite recourse to some relatively stern methods, could they stem in Germany the increasingly radical and violent student demonstrations that plagued all the Great Powers during the late 1960s. And when a mass-circulation magazine criticized certain "defects" in the armed forces, several of its executives were arrested for treason. As a consequence, some of the CDU's allies withdrew from the governing coalition in 1966—whereupon a strange new bloc was formed, including the CDU and the Social Democrats. The latter's leader, Willy Brandt, became foreign minister. After the elections of 1969, Brandt, as head of the largest party, became chancellor. His was the first Social Democratic government in Germany since 1930.

Brandt promptly sought conciliation with the Iron Curtain bloc. In bilateral treaties signed in 1970, with Russia and Poland, respectively, the use of force to settle disputes was renounced, and the "inviolability" of existing European boundaries was acknowledged. Ratification was delayed until 1972, at which time a new four-power agreement on Berlin, more or less restating the original occupation terms, also was ratified.

During the following year, the two German governments ratified a "Basic Treaty on Relations." Evading the issue of diplomatic recognition, it provided for the exchange of "permanent representative missions," rather than of ambassadors. The signatories promised to develop good relations, expressed mutual respect for existing frontiers, and forecast negotiations for cooperation in a variety of humanitarian and practical fields. Shortly thereafter, still in 1973, both West Germany and East Germany were admitted to membership in the United Nations.

These and other manifestations of Brandt's "softness" toward the Communists, and the openly leftist orientation of some of his chief advisers, led to heavy Socialist losses in the provincial elections of 1973. And when, in May, 1974, it was revealed that an active East German army officer for some time had been serving on Brandt's staff, the chancellor resigned.

His successor, former Defense Minister Helmut Schmidt, was an autocratic spellbinder who once had said that to be Marxist is not necessarily to be Communistic. It soon became apparent that, perhaps somewhat more suavely, he was following Brandt's policies, to the extent even of reappointing some of his predecessor's Leftist cabinet members. He also pushed welfare legislation, greatly enlarged the federal bureaucracy, and secured sizable pay increases for the expanding but economically unproductive civil service. Unemployment and inflation increased, though at a slower rate than elsewhere in the West and Japan. It was not astonishing, therefore, that the provincial elections in 1974 should continue to reflect a voter trend from the Social Democrats to the Christian Democrats.

In the Soviet zone, during these years, the situation resembled that in Russia and the other satellites. After the Communists lost the election of 1946, they took control by force and suspended further free elections. Then, after the declaration of the German Democratic Republic and the promulgation of a Soviet-style constitution in 1949, electors were given the opportunity to vote only for a single, official list of candidates.

Reconstruction of the war-ravaged area occurred within the framework of a series of five-year plans, the first having been launched in 1951. But the attempt to develop heavy industry in a traditionally agricultural region was hampered by many natural and human obstacles. As in Russia itself, moreover, there was a constant shortage of consumer goods. Gradually, private ownership was abolished, and the state so formulated its educational policy as to rear the youth in an atmosphere of materialism and atheism. The reaction of hundreds of thousands of Germans to all this was "to vote with their feet," that is, to flee to West Germany.

In June, 1953, to the dismay of Head of State Walter Ulbricht and his Russian masters, thousands of East Berliners went on strike and resorted to violence. The catalyst for the riots, aside from a food shortage, was the government's decree that individual labor productivity must be increased without correspondingly higher wages. Russian armor eventually subdued the uprising and life went on as before, marked by oppression, cultural drought, economic insufficiency and shoddy construction work, and lively police activity.

By 1960, all workers were assigned to jobs without regard to their preferences, child labor was encouraged, and industrialization was given an extra push at the expense of consumer goods. The government also strove, with relatively little success, to stamp out the staunch Lutheranism of the older populace. As a consequence of all this, more than 103,000 citizens fled to West Germany during the first half of 1961, with another 52,000 getting out in July and August of that year.*

Suddenly, then, on August 31, 1961, Russia closed the border between the two Germanies and started work on a concrete wall topped

---

*Between 1948 and 1973, the total population of East Germany fell from 20,000,000 to 17,000,000. During the same period, West Germany's population went up from 45,000,000 to 60,000,000.

with barbed wire and watchtowers to separate East from West Berlin. Eventually, the wall became twenty-eight miles long, and during the ensuing years, scores of East Germans were shot while trying to smuggle themselves to the West and freedom.

The Berlin Wall and closed border also gradually affected economic life within the German Democratic Republic. Sealed off from Western influences, East Germany had to foster its own economic development, and with the innate German tendency to work hard and efficiently, the country eventually became the industrial leader among Russia's satellites. Ulbricht cleverly used the "carrot-and-stick" policy of rewards and punishments and ordained that young people with talent be weaned from home influences by special and even lavish treatment. In 1968, the republic adopted a new constitution, which fit its complete Sovietization. In that year, too, East German forces assisted in the Soviet invasion of Czechoslovakia.

As Ulbricht, born in 1893, became older and less energetic, he was forced out of the top party office in 1971 and succeeded by Erich Honecker. The latter favored an easing of tension in Europe generally and friendlier relations with West Germany in particular. Internally, however, the state further strengthened its hold on the life of the individual—a process probably made the easier by the continued stationing in the German Democratic Republic of twenty-two Soviet army divisions.

THE OLD ORDER CHANGETH

HOPE SPRINGS ETERNAL

TOUCHSTONE AT THE SUMMIT

'THIS TRICK I KNOW WELL — WHEN DO WE TRY SOMETHING NEW?'

'THEY'RE MAKING PROGRESS – THEY AGREE TO DISAGREE AGAIN!'

FEAT OF CLAY

By L. D. Warren

"I DON'T FEEL A THING!"   —By L. D. Warren

THIS IS WHERE WE CAME IN   —By L. D. Warren

TALE OF TWO CITIES

'NUTHIN' - WHAT'S NEW WITH YOU?'

103

'AND PEACE-LOVING KHRUSHCHEV WON'T EVEN LET US VISIT OUR RELATIVES!'

'YESTERDAY WE HAD A POTATO WITH OUR HORSEMEAT!'

'MAY I BE NEXT? PLEASE, MISTER?'

PEACEFUL COEXISTENCE

105

'YOU'RE IN LUCK, BROTHER — THEY'VE AGREED TO LET ME VISIT YOU IN YOUR CELL!'

HUMPTY DUMPTY

'RUN ALONG AND PLAY – BUT DON'T GET DIRTY!'

GERMAN MEASLES

EAST GERMANY 1953

EAST GERMANY 1961

DENIED BALLOTS — THEY VOTE WITH THEIR HANDS — OR FEET

RED TROOPS

"FREEDOM"

EAST GERMANY

"YOU STILL NEED A BODYGUARD-MISTER!"

'DON'T TAKE IT SO HARD, WALTER — YOU'RE STILL AS FAITHFUL AS ANY DOG!'

"WHY DON'T YOU TWO GET TOGETHER?"

DOG'S BEST FRIEND

'GRANDMOTHER... I HOPE YOU'RE NOT HUNGRY, I BROUGHT YOU SOMETHING TO READ!'

6

ITALY

After freeing Rome from Nazi occupation in June, 1944, the Allies permitted pre-Fascist Italian leaders gradually to resume governmental control. The most radical resistance groups were dissolved, and a relatively conservative assembly was chosen in September, 1945, headed by the Christian Democrat, Alcide de Gasperi. Postwar reconstruction, with Allied help, assumed priority over all other programs. By the close of 1946, the Allies, chiefly the United States, had given the country half-a-billion dollars' worth of supplies. Thereafter, Marshall Plan aid was forthcoming, aimed at helping the economy in a way to raise the status of the workers and peasants.

A referendum in 1946 replaced the monarchy with a republic, and a new constitution was drafted in 1947. It was the handiwork of moderates and provided for a traditional parliamentary setup, with a president to be chosen by the bicameral parliament. The two houses were given approximately equal power. The Communists, excluded from representation in the new de Gasperi cabinet, became increasingly disruptive in their public activities and gradually added to their following some members of the Left fringe of the Socialist party.

The elections of 1948 brought a comfortable victory to the Christian Democrats, who were friendly to the Roman Catholic church and adopted a strongly pro-Western attitude. De Gasperi continued to function as premier, but in the ensuing years found it increasingly difficult to solve Italy's economic and social problems, all the more since factionalism developed within his party. The elections of 1953 sharply reduced his parliamentary influence. A succession of other Christian Democratic premiers came to depend more and more on coalitions with small Rightist groups in order to prevent a Communist takeover.

The monotonous rise and fall of cabinets made it virtually impossible for the administrations to make positive gains in economic development and improvement of the condition of the impoverished masses. Following the elections of 1963, the Christian Democrats formed a series of governing coalitions with the moderate Socialists, but still failed to function effectively. Again and again much-needed and oft-promised reforms in agriculture, education, and housing were postponed while the parliamentary delegates wasted time in acrimonious debate and stalling tactics. Disorder grew parallel with the progress of an inflationary spiral.

New elections in 1968 did little to resolve the Moderate-Leftist tug-of-war, and in August, 1970, Italy acquired its thirty-second government since the fall of Mussolini. For a time, in 1971-1972, the republic existed for nine months without a formal government, and during the next two years four more cabinets rose and fell. As one observer put it, the Italians, particularly the talkative, hair-splitting parliamentarians, appeared to prefer a "happy anarchy" to stable government.

To a considerable extent, the legislative stalemate reflected the conflicting interests of the industrial North and the backwardly agrarian South, a dichotomy that had plagued the country since its unification in 1870. The severe fighting in Italy during World War II between the Germans and the Allies, moreover, had resulted in paralyzing damage to such transportation links as highways, railroads, and bridges, and to factories. Nor was the republic happily endowed with natural resources. Marshall Plan technical assistance and money ($5,600,000,000 from 1947 to 1961), and the formation in 1952 of the European Coal and Steel Community (ECSC) with Italy as a member, did help. But in the long run, and in part because of widespread corruption, the gap widened between the few who were rich and the many who were poor.

The root difficulty in postwar Italy was the existence of too many people in a country with limited arable land and few natural resources. Those who lived in the industrial "iron triangle," with Milan, Turin, and Genoa at its points, were better off than those in any other area; the Sicilians were especially impoverished. The traditional Italian pressure outlet of emigration to the United States was clogged by American restrictions, and so there came about an active movement of Southerners to the North, not always with happy consequences. Indeed, as was the case with the Southern Blacks who moved northward in the United States, so the Italian wanderers generally found their hopes and dreams of a better life ending in disappointment. And so, gradually, the Italian Communist party grew to be the largest in Western Europe.

The peace treaty of 1947 and certain resolutions of the United Nations deprived Italy of all her former colonies. The Allies, however, permitted Rome to retain control over the still largely German-speaking South Tirol, renamed Alto-Adige, with resultant unrest and strained relations with Austria, which had been the former homeland of the Tirolese. In foreign policy, Italy generally was aligned with the West, hoping thus to reach a position of respect and prestige in world affairs. This effort, too, met with little success.

Although Italy became a member of NATO in 1949, she never was able to provide the promised twelve divisions to the organization's joint forces;

actually, as late as 1963, the whole Italian army consisted of only six full divisions. The establishment of the Common Market through the Treaty of Rome in 1957, with Italy as a founding member, raised hopes of better times. But the republic could not "pull its weight" economically even with the gradual elimination of tariffs among the Common Market members and with the large infusion of grants and loan funds from the Common Market and individual member states. By the end of 1974, and despite the able and devoted leadership of President Giovanni Leone, Italy was close to bankruptcy.

Because of history and the location of the Vatican, Italy had more direct relations with the Papacy than did other Catholic countries. During the years to 1958, the atmosphere generally was cordial. The Vatican supported the Christian Democratic policies, and Rome supported the Pope's efforts to uphold Catholic Christianity behind the Iron Curtain. A gradual change came about, however, after the death of the relatively tradition-minded Pope Pius XII in 1958.

His successor, Pope John XXIII, was an innovator whose relatively liberal pronouncements and actions did not satisfy the anticlericals and caused concern to some of the conservative Catholics. He continued Pius XII's precedent-breaking policy of keeping a non-Italian majority in the College of Cardinals, and appointed a number of African and Asiatic Cardinals. He frequently spoke out for disarmament and peace throughout the world and presided over the Ecumenical Church Council in 1962, which liberalized a number of rites and procedures. The Council also adopted the first major change in the mass since the seventh century.

The next pontiff, Paul VI, who was chosen in 1963, was the first since 1814 to leave Italy for foreign visits. He tried to effect a reconciliation with the Eastern or Greek Orthodox church, pleaded for an end to anti-Semitism, and urged the granting of religious liberty to all everywhere. In the much-talked-about matters of divorce and artificial birth-control, on the other hand, he clung to the traditional position of the Church. This aroused considerable criticism among Catholics abroad as well as at home, especially among women. The legalization of divorce by the Parliament in 1971 and the upholding of the law in a national referendum, both against the strenuous opposition of the Papacy, plus continuing agitation for voluntary birth-control and legalized abortion, provided additional fuel for unrest and turbulence.

REHEARSAL
—By L. D. Warren

NO MAN'S LAND
—By L. D. Warren

THE HANDS THAT ROCK THE CRADLE —By L. D. Warren

ELEVATOR SHOE —By L. D. Warren

MOSCOW TOOLS

—By L. D. Warren

"I Can Lick Any Man In The House!" —By L. D. Warren

—By L. D. Warren

"BUT WHY ISN'T IT LEANING?"

7

THE SOVIET UNION

Following victory in 1945, Moscow pursued reconstruction simultaneously along three fronts: economic, political, and ideological. Marxist-Leninist doctrine was reemphasized. National patriotism was stressed. The populace was kept in a state of uneasiness by recurrent warnings of the threat of American nuclear power. Machinery and virtually every other movable resource was expropriated from the occupied areas. Rewards for achievement and punishment for failure were widely publicized. The Union's own natural resources and manufacturing capability were developed vigorously, particularly east of the Ural Mountains.

The resulting progress was so significant as to make possible the allocation of large sums to intensive nuclear research, especially on the part of captured German scientists. As a consequence, the first Russian thermonuclear device was detonated in 1949. The production of consumer goods, on the other hand, was relegated to secondary importance.

For eight years after World War II, the Union's whole life course was determined and controlled by the dictatorial aims, whims, and suspicions of Joseph V. Stalin. He upheld his power by means of an intimidating secret-police force, a large army, a vast bureaucracy, and heavy censorship. This last, incidentally, was responsible for a prolonged stultification of Russia's literary output.

Stalin's absolutism made him the sole tangible symbol of Soviet hegemony. Upon his death in March, 1953, accordingly, the Communist party, having become wary of "cultism," experimented with a *troika* (group of three) system of collective leadership. Understandably, however, human nature being what it is, there soon developed a fierce struggle for primacy among the leading heirs of Stalin. By mid-1958, it was apparent that Nikita S. Khrushchev eventually would emerge as the new dictator.

Khrushchev was a shrewd, crude, and ruthless Ukrainian peasant who, in the 1930s, had carried out a number of Stalin-decreed political purges. During World War II, he had been a successful partisan fighter and leader. After the war, he rebuilt the Ukraine economically, effectively centralized all Soviet agricultural planning, and served Stalin directly as an aide in the party headquarters in Moscow. Soon after Stalin's death, he became First Secretary of the Communist party, in which post he so maneuvered events as gradually to remove from Moscow, apparently without executions, his main rivals. From 1958 to 1964, as both party secretary and premier, he exercised sole leadership of the Soviet Union.

In domestic affairs, Khrushchev briskly reorganized and centralized the Union's industrial structure and fostered the energetic development of Siberia's natural wealth. In foreign affairs, he adopted an "advance-recede policy," alternately being loudly aggressive and encouraging a "thaw" in the Cold War. On his foreign trips he alternated rough good nature and outright abusiveness.

By 1964, when Khrushchev reached seventy, it was evident that his tenure was becoming shaky. Domestic production was lagging, there was a renewed and potentially dangerous Sino-Soviet flare-up, and there was a growing fear among satellite countries of a possible split in world Communism. In October, Khrushchev was deposed from the premiership and deprived of all party offices on charges of economic ineptitude, boastfulness, and willfulness. Sent to live in the Crimea, he was succeeded by Leonid I. Brezhnev as head of the party and Aleksei N. Kosygin as premier.

Brezhnev, who changed the title of party leadership from First Secretary to General Secretary, seemed to work well with Kosygin. They loosened some of the earlier economic and political centralization, and promised greater emphasis on consumer goods as well as higher wages with which to purchase them. Gradually there came a noticeable improvement in the standard of living and in cultural opportunities for the masses.

Yet five-year plans to advance the production of capital goods while simultaneously making consumer goods more plentiful continued to be renewed into the 1970s, and state control over most aspects of the individual's life remained firm. Moreover, Moscow's fear that a spreading liberalism in satellite Czechoslovakia might infect other neighbors and, indeed, the people in the Union itself, led in 1968 to a brutal military invasion of the Central European republic and to a reestablishment of repression under Soviet auspices.

Despite or because of the continuing autocracy and censorship, there was mounting evidence, as the decade of the 1970s opened, of widespread dissent among writers, scientists, poets, and artists. Spearheading the movement for greater freedom of expression and a loosening of the police-state controls was the poet and novelist, Aleksandr I. Solzhenitsyn. Among the best known of Russian writers to the outside world, he was awarded the Nobel Prize for his voluminous and documented critique of the evils of Soviet dictatorship entitled *Gulag Archipelago* (1973). Owing largely to strong foreign reaction, Solzhenitsyn, who several times had been imprisoned and sent to forced-labor camps, now (1974) was expelled rather than reimprisoned. He continued his exposés from his new abode in Switzerland.

In foreign relations, meanwhile, despite the existence of basically different stances in the worsening Arab-Israeli conflict and in the oil crisis precipitated in 1972 by the oil-producing countries, Brezhnev and President Nixon did fashion a détente in 1973-1974. This imbued with hope some who had feared the possibility of a nuclear confrontation triggered by some irresponsible act. It increased the concern of others, especially in the United States, who thought that Washington had made broad military and economic concessions without a substantive *quid pro quo.*

The developments in the Russian-dominated neighboring states generally paralleled those in the Soviet Union itself. As the Allies after World War I, largely at the insistence of a worried France, had set up a *cordon sanitaire* of new buffer states between Bolshevik Russia and the West, so now, after World War II, a worried Soviet Union created by force a group of satellite states reaching from the Baltic Sea to the Black Sea.

The domestic and foreign policies of the satellites perforce were patterned on those of Russia, for the countries were ruled by puppet Communist governments that received their instructions from Moscow. East Germany, Poland, Yugoslavia, Hungary, Romania, and Bulgaria all were drawn and, with one exception, kept behind the "Iron Curtain." Only Yugoslavia, under Joseph Tito, managed from 1948 onward to chart its own autonomous Communist course. And Communist Albania, controlled by Enver Hoxha, preferred to establish close relations with Communist China.

Anti-Soviet revolutionary outbreaks did occur in East Berlin (1953), Poland (1956), and Hungary (1956), but all were put down with heavy armaments and at the cost of much bloodshed. A sturdy liberalizing movement in Czechoslovakia, as has been indicated, was checked by an actual Soviet invasion in 1968. As in the case of Adolf Hitler's imperialistic aggressions several decades earlier, the concern of the Western democracies over these acts of Soviet imperialism was expressed chiefly in words.

MARXIST DOUBLE-HEADER

'NEED HELP IN MAKING UP YOUR MIND?'

"JUST HAVE A CHAIR, PLEASE—THE DOCTOR IS BUSY!"

'HOLD IT! DIDN'T SOMEONE CALL THE CORONER?'

THE FLAME THAT NEVER DIES

'YOU SAID, WELL DONE — DIDN'T YOU, MR. DUBCEK?'

'WOULD YOU MIND SLOWING DOWN, SIR — WHILE I RECOVER MY WHISTLE?'

128

'HAPPY ANNIVERSARY! NOW BLOW REAL HARD!'

'JUST LET ME GET MY HANDS ON THAT KID!'

'HEAVY-HEAVY-WHAT HANGS OVER?'

SHALLOW GRAVE

COLUMBUSCHEV UNCOVERS AMERICA

'SEE, COMRADES! I TOLD YOU COMMUNISM WOULD SURPASS CAPITALISM!'

'THE SOVIET ARMS IN CUBA ARE NOT OFFENSIVE!' — *PENTAGON*

— AND FAR INTO THE NIGHT

8

THE MIDDLE EAST*

Any effort to understand the troubled Middle East, and particularly the Arab-Israeli problem, must take into account certain historical facts. First, the Arabs, despite sometimes careless reporting, are not anti-Semitic, for they themselves admittedly are Semites. Most of them, however, have been strongly anti-Zionist and anti-Israel. In other words, they have been opposed to the establishment and continuance of a dominant Jewish political entity in Palestine, where, through the events of history, the Arabs far outnumbered the Jews in 1945. This opposition, in turn, fixed the basis of all Israeli foreign policy, namely, national survival.

Second, London, in 1917, in order to elicit the fullest possible aid of Jews at home and abroad during World War I, issued the Balfour Declaration. This one-paragraph document, interpreted differently by Jews and by Arabs, asserted that Great Britain, after the return of peace, would "view with favor the establishment in Palestine of a National Home for the Jews . . . , it being clearly understood that nothing shall be done which may prejudice the civil and religious rights of existing non-Jewish communities in Palestine. . . ." Beyond this, the Allies of World War I also promised self-determination and independence to all former Arabian subjects of the Ottoman Empire (of which Palestine then was a part). When Great Britain assumed administrative control of Palestine in 1922, the population of that League of Nations Mandate included some 600,000 Moslem Arabs, 73,000 Christian Arabs, and 83,000 Jews. Jerusalem, moreover, is regarded as a holy city by Christians, Jews, and Moslems.

Third, the picture was complicated, after 1945, by (a) the presence of vast oil (petroleum) reserves in the area; (b) the attractiveness to Moscow of the Middle East as a field for ideological and political expansion; and (c) the special political situation related to frequent national

---

*This term has had a variety of geographic meanings since the midnineteenth century. As here defined, it reflects current popular usage; that is, it encompasses Egypt, the Arabian Peninsula, and Iran.

elections in the United States. And now, let us turn to Egypt, which, after shedding British control, saw in the Israeli problem an opportunity to seek primacy among the Arabian nations.

During World War II, young Egyptian nationalists, particularly among the army officers, actually favored a German victory, expecting that thus the British would be ousted from their country. The special target of their ire was the Anglo-Egyptian Treaty of 1936. This document allowed London, which wanted to keep control of the Suez Canal area, to maintain a military force in the Cairo-Suez region.

After 1945, the government of King Farouk found the British ready to modify the treaty in Egypt's favor, but Egyptian public opinion opposed any arrangement other than departure of the foreign military. Farouk vainly hoped to lessen the tension by ordering elections in 1948. These were won by the nationalistic Wafd party, which promptly mounted guerrilla attacks against British troops. Gradually, the people turned, not alone against the foreigners, but against the king and the whole elitist social system.

Some of the young army officers now assumed a role not unlike that of earlier bourgeois revolutionaries in Europe. Lieutenant Colonel Gamel Abdel Nasser (1918-1970) organized a Free Officers' Committee and, in 1952, overthrew the cabinet, drove the luxury-loving Farouk into exile, and installed himself as premier. In June, 1953, the monarchy was abolished in favor of a republic, and Nasser became deputy premier and minister of the interior under the respected and more conservative President and Premier General Mohammed Naguib.

A program of "Arab Socialism" promptly was launched. Its aim was at breaking up large estates, reducing the dependence of the economy on cotton, fostering industrialization under government sponsorship, and establishing state control over the unions, the universities, the press, and other customarily liberal institutions. Plans were started for the building of the Aswan High Dam to irrigate an additional million acres of land.

Early in 1954, London agreed to withdraw from the Suez Canal Zone within two years. Shortly after evacuation began, Nasser ousted Naguib, made himself premier and head of state, and tackled the only remaining major challenge to his supremacy. This challenge came from the Moslem Brotherhood, which identified the new leadership with Western Liberalism. The premier moved swiftly and drastically by suppressing the Brotherhood, hanging some of its leaders following an attempt on his life, and converting the republic into a secular state. In 1956, a plebiscite elected him president, with dictatorial power.

During 1956, too, London and Washington showed their displeasure over Nasser's activity by withdrawing earlier offers to help finance construction of the Aswan Dam. Thereupon, Nasser nationalized the Suez operation and took possession of its Egyptian assets.* This step led to a hastily (and poorly) planned Anglo-Franco-Israeli invasion of Egypt in October-November, 1956. Before the attack achieved any important objective, except for an Israeli advance into the Sinai Desert, the invaders withdrew under strong pressure from President Eisenhower and the United Nations.

The outcome of this venture established Nasser as the "anticolonialist" hero of Africa, although he soon proved to have far more influence in the Middle East than on his own continent. In 1958, indeed, he persuaded Syria and then Yemen to join Egypt in a United Arab Republic (UAR) under his presidency. (Disillusioned with Nasser's efforts to dominate Syria and Yemen, Cairo's two partners left the federation in 1961; but Egypt held on to the name UAR until a new, loose federation of Arab republics came into being with Syria and Libya on New Year's Day, 1972.) Meanwhile, in 1958, the Soviet Union, despite Nasser's antipathy to Communism at home, advanced money to Egypt to start building the Aswan Dam and flooded the country with Soviet technicians.

Nasser's authoritarianism created some domestic discontent, but his adoption of a strong anti-Israeli stand was popular. Propaganda against Israel became a staple of the Cairo government, and a large share of the country's limited capital was diverted from economic to military development. The economic boycott against Israel also was intensified and, in June, 1967, as will be described later, he precipitated another war against the Jewish state.

When, in this war, Egypt, Syria, and Jordan were beaten, thousands of students and other young Egyptians began to demonstrate against Nasser's antidemocratic position—something that seemed not to have bothered them when their dictator seemed about to lead his people to greatness. At the same time, the youthful army officers again became restless and agitated for still another war against Israel. During the spring of 1970, accordingly, Nasser negotiated for Soviet help in the building of missile bases and for Soviet air support against Israeli reprisal raids. A few months later, the fifty-two-year-old Nasser died suddenly of a heart attack. He was succeeded by Vice President Anwar el-Sadat.

Meanwhile, the end of World War II had signaled the beginning of a seemingly insoluble problem of Palestine, a League of Nations Mandate under British rule since 1922. The Arabs in Palestine, promised self-determination by the Allies, had come to be fiercely nationalistic and

---

*This action of Nasser, and the later blocking of the Canal by sunken ships during the Arab-Israeli War of 1967, greatly increased the importance of South Africa's ports on the new, long oil-and cargo-vessel route around the Cape of Good Hope—the only alternative sea route between the West and East.

eager for independence. On the other hand, hundreds of thousands of Jewish refugees, who, as a consequence of World War II, had been stranded in various Mediterranean ports, wished to enter Palestine. Yet, they could do so only illegally, because the British in 1939 had tried to appease the Arabs by placing a strict quota on immigration into the Holy Land. Hence there occurred much smuggling of refugees, while armed Jewish bands fought the protesting Arabs.

So bitter did Arab-Jewish relations become that the British, unwilling to sacrifice any more of their soldiers to peace-keeping efforts, asked the United Nations to solve the problem. A plan of partition was evolved, in 1947, providing for a Jewish state, an Arabian state, and an internationalized Jerusalem. A commission appointed to carry out the proposal spent so much time talking in New York that London announced its decision to quit the area in May, 1948.

Thereupon, Jewish leaders in Tel Aviv declared the independence of the new Republic of Israel at midnight on May 14-15, 1948. The new state, with declared boundaries similar to those proposed in the partition plan, immediately was recognized by President Truman and Premier Stalin. The League of Arab States, founded in 1945 to boycott the Jews, now resorted to war, only to be soundly defeated. Israel, indeed, increased its limited area through conquest by about half.*

Israel's first president was Dr. Chaim Weizmann, the British-born scientist who had been instrumental in persuading London to issue the Balfour Declaration. David Ben-Gurion, a Polish-born labor leader and freedom fighter, became premier, holding that post, with a brief intermission, until 1963. After some years of leadership by Levi Eshkol, the premiership, in 1969, passed to Mrs. Golda Meir (Myerson), a Russian-born schoolteacher from Milwaukee. Born in 1898, she retired in 1974, and was succeeded by Major General Yitzhak Rabin.

Despite a continuing Arab economic boycott and frequent border raids, Israel prospered. Money from Washington and from private American and British sources, discipline and hard work, a high degree of literacy, scientific knowledge and ingenuity, a strong spirit of nationality, skill in irrigation, and the manpower of immigrants, all resulted in a remarkable strengthening of the small state. Some 700,000-800,000 Arabs were ousted for both security and land-use reasons. These impoverished refugees and their descendants received little help except from Western donations. Their continuing presence near Israel in the adjoining Arab

---

*The League of Arab States originally included Egypt, Iraq, Jordan, Lebanon, Saudi Arabia, Syria, and Yemen. In 1975, it had twenty members, stretching across Africa from Mauritania to Somalia, and from Syria to Oman and the United Arab Emirates on the Persian Gulf. Tunisia was conspicuous among the membership for favoring recognition of Israel.

states did not ease the tension in the Middle East. The population of Israel trebled between 1948 and 1974, and in the latter year was estimated at 3,350,000 (85 percent Jewish and 7 percent Moslem), with another 1,000,000 persons in the regions occupied after the Arab-Israeli War of 1967. Understandably, Israel's foreign policy continued to be dictated by her survival needs.

Nasser's nationalization of the Suez Canal and its subsequent closing to Israel, as well as frequent Arab border raids, led Israel to act with Great Britain and France in an invasion of Egypt in 1956. Under the leadership of the one-eyed Major General Moshe Dayan, the Israeli overran the Sinai Peninsula; pressure by the United Nations, however, led to early evacuation of the desert area. A decade later, after ceaseless harassment by Egyptian, Syrian, and Jordanian units, the Israeli, in the Six-Day War in June, 1967, defeated all three neighbors despite their great superiority in manpower and in (Russian-supplied) equipment.

This time, Israel conquered and remained in occupation of the Gaza Strip and Sinai Peninsula taken from Egypt, the Golan Heights from Syria, and the west bank of the Jordan River and the Old City of Jerusalem from Jordan. The occupied land covered 26,500 square miles— more than three times the area of Israel, and it improved the republic's border defensibility. The government almost immediately began to build roads and water facilities in the territories and to establish in them new Jewish settlements.

The United Nations adopted a resolution in November, 1967, asking Israel's withdrawal from the occupied regions in return for an Arabian acknowledgment of her sovereignty and independence within "secure and recognized boundaries." Inasmuch as each side demanded initial compliance by the other, the situation remained in stalemate. Although Jordan, ruled by King Hussein, adopted a moderate attitude and eliminated the Palestinian-Arab guerrilla bases on its soil, Egypt and Syria prepared for renewed fighting.

On October 6, 1973, on the Jewish high holy day of Yom Kippur, they launched the fourth Arab-Israeli war in twenty-eight years. This time, the Israeli were caught by surprise and suffered early setbacks. Within two weeks, however, they recovered and trapped an Egyptian army of 20,000 in the Sinai Desert. Both Washington and Moscow now used their influence to bring about a cease-fire, save the encircled Egyptian force, and even regain for Cairo and Damascus small portions of the areas they had lost in 1967.

Secretary of State Henry A. Kissinger then paid a long series of mediation visits to all involved Middle Eastern capitals in an effort to resolve the continuing dispute. But in March, 1975, he gave up in favor of renewed collective efforts at the Geneva Conference, of which the

United States and the Soviet Union were co-chairmen. Despite a public statement by Sadat that Egypt had become tired of Moscow's attempts of "guardianship" over Egypt, Soviet military supplies continued to flow to the Arabs—particularly to those who showed Leftist leanings—and the United States continued to send similar aid to Israel and to moderate Jordan.

Meanwhile, from the spring of 1970, some thousands of Palestinian Arabs, under the headship of Yassir Arafat, entered a Palestine Liberation Organization (PLO). Based originally in Jordan, but then in Syria and Lebanon, and supported by Egypt and Libya, the PLO was dedicated to the recovery of all Israeli-occupied territory and, seemingly, the actual destruction, by any and all means, of Israel as an independent state. The PLO carried on border raids; exploded bombs in buses, airports, and village squares; hijacked commercial planes, both Israeli and foreign; murdered eleven members of the Israeli Olympic team at the 1972 Munich games; bombed foreign embassies; took hostages for the release from captivity of fellow-terrorists; and the like. In October, 1974, the Afro-Arabian bloc in the United Nations General Assembly gave a seat to the PLO and invited Arafat to speak. Gleefully he announced that he was carrying an olive branch in one hand and a gun in the other.

When none of this led to Israeli collapse, the Arabs cleverly took advantage, in October, 1973, of the dependence of the West and Japan on Arabian oil for their energy requirements by raising the price of crude oil sevenfold and, temporarily, placing an embargo on oil shipments to several countries, including the United States. Non-Arabian oil producers, such as Iran and Venezuela, soon followed suit. Wholly aside from the personal hardship caused to hundreds of millions by this policy, severe economic damage was done to the West and Japan, with resulting inflation, widespread unemployment, and a decline in international trade. Then, using as a lever their newfound wealth, which was measured in billions of dollars and whose reinvestment eagerly was sought in the tight money markets of the West, the Arabs began "blacklisting" foreign firms that did business with Israel or that had Jewish officers or directors. Perhaps the fundamental block to peace in the Middle East was, as one British official in the days of the mandate is said to have remarked, the absence in both the Arabic and Israeli tongues of an expression for "compromise."

Most powerful among the Middle Eastern countries three decades after the close of World War II was the 2500-year-old Empire of Iran, known, until 1935, as Persia. Its estimated population in 1974 of about 32,000,000 was largely Moslem—non-Arabian racially, but pro-Arabian in sympathy. Its ruler since 1941 has been Mohammed Reza Shah Pahlavi, a well-educated, enlightened, decisive man, admirer of Western technology and efficiency. He was just under twenty-two when he ascended the throne, following his father's abdication—an abdication brought about as a wartime measure by Great Britain and Russia because of the ruler's pro-Nazi leanings.

During the first five years of his reign, the young Shah was virtually powerless. The Allies needed, and used, the country as a supply route for getting (largely American) equipment to Russia, and Tehran had no choice in the matter. The British withdrew soon after the Axis surrendered, but the Russians stayed on. Meanwhile, Iran's economy had been dislocated, and a strong national spirit had developed among the people.

In 1946, Iran brought to the United Nations one of the latter's earliest cases, namely, Moscow's continuing interference in the internal affairs of a foreign state. The Soviets tried unsuccessfully to prevent consideration of the dispute, and then recalled their troops.

The next quinquennium, until 1951, saw the Iranian government dominated by an extreme nationalist, a forceful and powerful landholder named Dr. Mohammed Mossadegh. He exercised dictatorial authority as premier and strove to curtail the previously granted oil rights of several Western states; but he was unable to deal effectively with a critical economic situation. The Shah, supported by the army, dismissed Mossadegh in 1956, and thereafter ruled as well as reigned.

Mohammed Reza redistributed the land, stimulated the cultivation in export quantity of fruit and cotton, encouraged textile manufacture, introduced compulsory education, insisted on profit-sharing in the developing industries, extended the suffrage to women in national elections, and submitted a number of social proposals to referenda. As did so many other countries, so did Iran launch a series of five-year plans.

In foreign affairs, during the score of years to 1970, the Shah faced an alternating policy of threats and blandishments by the Russians; thereafter, having made Iran much stronger, he reacted more cordially toward Soviet economic and technical overtures. But, as Iran gradually broke away from her traditional stance of nonalignment, she firmly committed herself to a pro-Western policy. This resulted in steadily mounting United States aid, including modern weaponry and technical instructors.

Although sympathetic to Moslem causes, Tehran generally maintained a neutral position in the Arab-Israeli dispute. With neighboring Iraq, moreover, there were frequent clashes along the ill-defined boundaries, and the Iranians appeared sympathetic to the Kurds who rebelled against Baghdad. When Great Britain, in 1971, gave up her long-term occupation of some Arabian territory along the Persian Gulf, Iran promptly established her own control over the area.

Even in the matter of petroleum politics, the Shah pursued an essentially independent course. He gradually nationalized the foreign oil operations and then, at a high price, sold the oil to the companies that had developed the wells and fields. In 1971, alone, it was estimated that Iran made a net profit of two billion dollars through the arrangement. In 1972, Iran dissociated herself from the Organization of Petroleum Exporting Countries (OPEC) that it had helped found in 1960. The Shah then conducted more satisfactory negotiations with the West on his own, negotiations based on world economics and Iranian welfare rather than on the basis of vengeance and retribution.

SILENT NIGHT

—By L. D. Warren

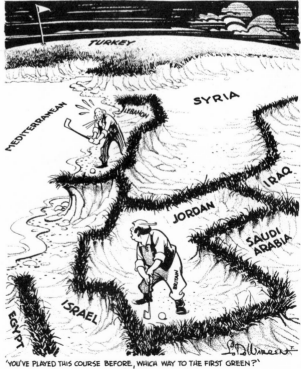

'YOU'VE PLAYED THIS COURSE BEFORE, WHICH WAY TO THE FIRST GREEN?'

'YOU'RE THIRSTY ?'

LITTLE EGYPT

"HERE'S YOUR HAT - WHAT'S YOUR HURRY?"

"WHO NEEDS A PLUMBER?"

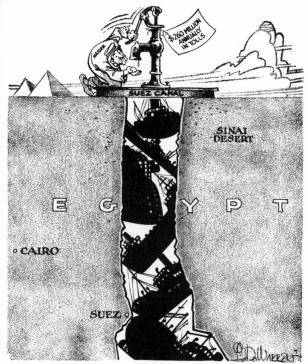

YOU NEVER MISS IT, UNTIL IT RUNS DRY

EYEBALL TO EYEBALL

'MMM — NASTY LEAK YOU HAVE HERE!'

'YOU ARE GOING TO LEAVE YOUR TOOLS, AREN'T YOU?'

'MY UNCLE CAN LICK YOUR UNCLE!'

'WHY DON'T YOU WATCH WHERE YOU'RE DRIVING?'

THE LAND OF MILK AND HONEY

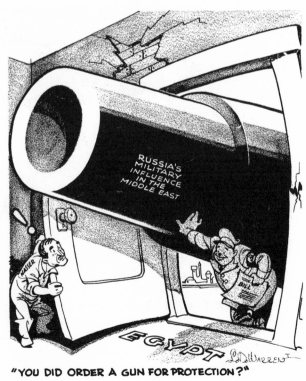

"YOU DID ORDER A GUN FOR PROTECTION?"

"WHY DON'T YOU WATCH WHERE YOU'RE GOING?"

'THINK FAST!'

153

'WATCH CLOSELY, YOUNG LADY... I'LL TELL YA WHAT I'M GONNA DO!'

'ON YOUR MARK! GET SET! ---'

154

'I WON'T GET OUT 'TIL YOU GO AWAY!' 'I WON'T GO AWAY 'TIL YOU GET OUT!'

'I CAN LICK ANY MAN IN THE HOUSE! CARRY ME BACK IN ... FOR THE FOURTH TIME!'

'MAKE ME!'

ARAB
THREATS

MIDEAST
OIL

SCAVENGERS' ROOST

TIME MARCHES ON

SWORD OF DAMOCLES.

—By L. D. Warren

UN ENFORCEMENT

DECEMBER 11, 1947

CEASE-FIRE LINE

GOLAN HEIGHTS

MEDITERRANEAN SEA

JORDAN WEST BANK

ISRAEL

SINAI PENINSULA

'IT WAS BAD ENOUGH WHEN IT USED TO BE A LITTLE SWORD!'

'IT'S A BIT SMALL, BUT WE'LL DRIVE IT FOR FIVE YEARS THEN TRADE IT FOR A BIGGER MODEL!'

WISHING WELL

MIDNIGHT OIL

'OOPS, SORRY 'BOUT THAT! COULD I INTEREST YOU IN RELIABLE FIRE INSURANCE?'

ALL THE KING'S MEN ---

STILL NO ROOM AT THE INN

9

INDIA, PAKISTAN, BANGLADESH

The Labor government that took office in Great Britain in 1945 moved promptly to grant independence to India. The chief obstacle encountered during the necessary negotiations was the age-old split between Hindus and Moslems along the lines of religion, language, and political outlook. The large and relatively homogeneous Moslem minority favored a religious state. The Hindu majority was much more diversified in stock and language, and its political leaders generally favored a secular government. The only practical solution appeared to be a division of the subcontinent, and such an arrangement was included in London's Indian Independence Act of 1947.

The law sanctioned the creation of a (Hindu) Commonwealth of India and a (Moslem) Commonwealth of Pakistan, meaning "Land of the Pure." Inasmuch as the populations in many areas were intermingled, it was necessary to draw compromise boundaries. Pakistan, indeed, was made up of two sections: East Pakistan and West Pakistan, with a nearly 1000-mile stretch of Indian territory between them.

Some 10,000,000 fear-filled refugees tried to cross from one new commonwealth to the other, and in the process an estimated 600,000 lost their lives. Even so, more than 11 percent of the people remaining in the new India were Moslems, and the Hindus formed a minority of perhaps 25 percent in Pakistan. Several hundred autonomous states under their own princes were given the option of joining either commonwealth, and most chose India.

In India, the assassination by a Hindu extremist of the long-time Hindu leader, Mohandas K. Gandhi, in 1948, added to the difficulty of establishing a new government. The then 340,000,000 inhabitants were grouped in thirty states. (By 1973, the population had increased to 580,000,000, living in a reorganized Union of twenty-one states and two territories.) The constitution of 1950 forbade discrimination against the "untouchable caste" in public places, stressed the need for general education and decent working conditions, and established a bicameral parliamentary system. The president was made a figurehead, whereas the prime minister was invested with considerable power. The judiciary was made independent. Federally-appointed governors were to administer the states. Among Gandhi's successors, the most effective were Prime Minister Jawaharlal Nehru (1947-1964) and his daughter, Indira Gandhi, who came to power in 1966.

The dominant and moderate Congress party carried out the social mandates of the constitution so slowly that several radical parties began to attract sizable followings. Eventually, however, the rights of the land-lords over the peasantry were restricted, some land was redistributed, and industrialization was fostered. The government itself, from the out-set, monopolized and expanded the manufacture of armaments.

The first of a series of five-year plans to increase food production, control floods, improve transportation, and stimulate light and heavy industry, was inaugurated in 1947. The succeeding plans transferred much of heavy industry to the public sector, and placed added emphasis on education in the hundreds of thousands of villages that had no schools. Famine, however, remained endemic; and illiteracy, amounting to 85 percent in 1951, still was at 70 percent ten years later.

Population growth, moreover, despite official propaganda for birth control, continued to outstrip economic growth, and several "crash programs" aimed at improving the life of the masses were ineffectual. Essentially, neither domestic efforts to improve agricultural methods nor the annual importation of millions of tons of grain (often as gifts from the United States) were sufficient to feed the hungry, as long as the latter, for religious reasons, fed hundreds of millions of cows before they fed themselves and refused to kill these "sacred" animals for food. (On the other hand, impoverished but prestige-hungry India found the money necessary to explode her first nuclear device in 1974.)

As the 1960s drew to a close, Indira Gandhi faced serious opposition within her own party. In 1969, indeed, her candidate for the presidency of the Congress party narrowly escaped defeat. Gradually, therefore, she began to rely on help from the Communist and other Leftist parties. After India's victory over Pakistan in the war of 1971 (see below), the premier enjoyed a brief revival of popularity, and the elections of 1971 for the lower house and of 1972 for the upper house increased the size of the Congress party's parliamentary delegations. But then the effects of a severe drought and Mrs. Gandhi's personal desire for closer relations with Moscow brought renewed opposition within her party and a conse-quent strengthening of her alliance with Communist elements.

In foreign affairs, India continued to value the economic advantages of membership in the British Commonwealth, and sought prestige as the largest "neutralist" power between the Communist and anti-Communist blocs. (On occasion, she was not above playing off the committed powers against one another.) In 1956, New Delhi persuaded Paris to cede to India centuries-old French possessions such as Pondicherry, and in 1961 used force to oust the Portuguese from Goa. The most serious and prolonged foreign quarrels were with Red China over boundary delineations and with Pakistan over the beautiful land of Kashmir.

The Indochinese boundary dispute began, at Chinese instigation, in 1957, and was made worse when, in 1959, New Delhi gave sanctuary to the Dalai Lama after Peking, in traditional imperialist fashion, forcibly annexed Tibet. Three years later, the Chinese, against virtually no opposition, pushed some eighty miles into northeastern India. After the United States responded generously to New Delhi's appeal for material aid, Peking agreed to a cease-fire and withdrew its forces. Thereafter, the Red Chinese continued to keep things restless along a thousand-mile border and, through propaganda and diplomacy, fomented the already bad feelings between India and Pakistan.

In 1947, wealthy and renowned Kashmir, in the western Himalayas, was ruled by its own maharajah. Seventy percent of the inhabitants were Moslems, who long had been oppressed by a Hindu elite. When tens of thousands of Hindu refugees from the new Pakistan fled to Kashmir, Moslem tribesmen from the north moved southward. Disturbed by the resulting violence, the maharajah appealed to New Delhi for help, promising, in turn, to merge his land with India.

Eventually, the dispute was referred to the United Nations, which proposed a withdrawal of both Moslem tribesmen and Hindu soldiers, followed by a plebiscite. India feared the result of such a referendum and, instead, persuaded the maharajah in 1952 to sign a treaty of affiliation, short of incorporation. Five years later, imitating the imperialist tactics about which it long had chided the West, India simply announced the full integration of three-fifths of Kashmir.

Red China, then, having, as we have seen, both invaded and withdrawn from India in 1962, troubled the waters once more in 1963, by recognizing Pakistan's claims to Kashmir. Two years later, India attacked the Moslems in Kashmir, but in the following year, 1966, signed the Declaration of Tashkent, agreeing to another truce. This and several later armistices and cease-fire agreements were violated as regularly as they were accepted. Eventually, with other factors, the dispute over Kashmir and one over East Pakistan led to an outright Pakistani-Indian war that had dire results for the Moslem state.

At the time of its birth in 1947, Pakistan, with more than 70,000,000 people, was the seventh largest country in the world. (By 1971, the population had risen to an estimated 93,000,000.) Inasmuch as the first significant call for an independent Islamic state had not been issued until seven years earlier, Pakistan's leaders had had little time to prepare for the mechanics of independence. Undaunted, the heads of the Moslem

League, chief rival of the Congress party in the old India, quickly set up a makeshift governmental structure. This envisioned eventual democracy but of necessity extended current dominant authority to Mohammed Ali Jinnah, head of the Moslem League and of the newly elected Constituent Assembly.

Jinnah died in 1948, and a series of successors was unable to keep order, establish a stable government, or provide sufficient food. (The United States, Australia, and Canada donated some hundreds of thousands of tons of wheat to alleviate the hunger.) For these reasons, and because the Moslem League tended to reflect the interests of the large landholders more than those of the peasantry, the elections of 1954 and 1956 in East and West Pakistan, respectively, went against the government. Continuing instability and starvation led President Iskander Mirza, in 1958, to suspend parliament and appoint a "strong man," Mohammed Ayub Khan, as premier. A few weeks later, Ayub assumed the presidency as well, abolished political parties, and made himself dictator.

Ayub restored order, fought political corruption, and effectively stimulated advances in agriculture and industry. Next, the populace was given opportunity to learn democratic ways by being permitted to elect local governing councils. Thereafter, higher councils were chosen indirectly, or, at the top, were appointed. In 1962, then, a new constitution extended universal suffrage for the election of an 80,000-member (later 120,000-member) electoral college, which in turn was to choose the members of the national assembly and the president. Political parties were permitted to re-form, the most important one again being the Moslem League, which supported Ayub. In 1965, he was reelected president for a five-year term.

Pakistan, like India, was faced with the dual difficulty of low living standards and a rapidly growing population. The first of a number of five-year plans was inaugurated in 1955; they all were aimed at reducing the people's dependence on the land by emphasizing industrialism—a development that also would strengthen the country's military potential. Large landholdings were broken up and very small ones were consolidated to create units that might be farmed more efficiently. With foreign aid, factories and industrial plants were established, and the government urged peasant families to move to the cities. There *was* some improvement in the lot of the average citizen, but here, too, population growth was faster than economic growth.

The government meanwhile tried to cooperate closely with Great Britain and the United States, and joined several international defensive organizations. The underlying motive always was to attract and hold friends in the event of a full-scale clash with India and its sixfold advantage in manpower. When, after the Chinese invasion of India, London and Washington backed New Delhi, the Pakistani turned to Peking for diplomatic support. And soon after President Ayub's election in 1965, the Kashmir dispute with India led to his downfall.

Former Foreign Minister Zulfikar Ali Bhutto, who was strongly pro-Chinese (though not Communist) in outlook, broke with Ayub because of the latter's relatively moderate position on Kashmir and his acceptance of the 1966 Tashkent truce with India. In 1967, Bhutto formed the opposition Pakistani People's party and toured West Pakistan, making violent speeches demanding the "liberation" of Kashmir. He so aroused the populace that an attempt was made to assassinate Ayub and the disorder became riotous. Ayub resigned in 1969, and control was assumed by General Agha Mohamad Yahya Khan. The latter proclaimed martial law, made himself president, and promised soon to hold elections for a new constitutional assembly.

Yahya Khan called the elections toward the close of 1970, but remained in office for only another year. Long-standing dissatisfaction in East Pakistan (peopled largely by Bengali) with the alleged oppressiveness of the government that was headquartered in West Pakistan (first at Rawalpindi and then in the newly constructed Islamabad) broke into open resistance early in 1971. When Yahya ordered strong action against the dissidents, the Bengali issued a declaration of independence in March and proclaimed the new state of Bangladesh or "Bengal Nation."

India, seizing the opportunity to diminish her Islamic neighbor, promptly sent large military forces to aid the Bengali Nationalists in the resulting war. The Pakistani army in East Pakistan was badly beaten and surrendered in mid-December, 1971. Three days later, Bhutto ousted Yahya and made himself President and Chief Martial Law Administrator. But the land he administered was limited to the former West Pakistan.

In the summer of 1972, Indira Gandhi and Bhutto met at Simla and agreed to settle all outstanding issues between their countries peaceably. Then, with turmoil continuing in both Bangladesh and Kashmir, implementation of much of the Simla Agreement was held up into 1974, largely because of demands made by Bangladesh. The Bengali asked India to hold in prison camps some 93,000 Pakistani military and civilian prisoners of war until Dacca could decide on whom it wished to prosecute as "war criminals" and until Pakistan officially recognized the new state's independence. Islamabad, in turn, refused to allow perhaps 150,000-200,000 Bengali to emigrate from Pakistan to Bangladesh. The Kashmir dispute, however, was settled, at least temporarily, when Bhutto and Gandhi agreed to "respect" a new cease-fire line which divided Kashmir so that India annexed outright three-fifths of the region. (Early in 1975, Sheikh Mohammed Abdullah, who had "ruled" Kashmir during all the years of the dispute since 1948, and who now became chief minister of the Kashmir state, stated that the merger was "final and irrevocable." Pakistan, however, promptly denied the finality.)

Bhutto and his middle-of-the-road Pakistani People's party continued in control of the new Pakistan, with its population estimated in 1973 at 65,000,000. Mass poverty remained the chief domestic problem, and Bhutto now sought help chiefly from both Russia and China. In 1972, indeed, Pakistan showed its displeasure with the West by leaving the British Commonwealth of Nations.

Bangladesh, with its capital at Dacca and a population estimated in 1973 at 75,000,000, came under the presidency, and then the premiership, of Sheikh Mujibur Rahman, who recently had suffered imprisonment for his nationalistic agitation. The new republic embarked on an essentially Socialist program, promptly nationalizing banks, insurance companies, and the major industries, and breaking up the large landholdings. After Red China in 1972 vetoed Bangladesh's application for United Nations membership, Dacca drew closely to Russia. There was, however, a strong and growing Maoist movement, feeding on the governmental inefficiency and corruption and the starvation that gripped the land, particularly after a series of disastrous floods in 1973. (Early in 1975, Rahman proclaimed the country a one-party state—that party being his newly formed Peasants', Laborers', and People's League.)

MOTHER INDIA

—By L. D. Warren

AFGHANISTAN

BALUCHISTAN

TIBET

NEPAL

RACIAL AND RELIGIOUS STRIFE

ARABIAN SEA

BAY OF BENGAL

THE MOUNTAIN THAT CAME TO MAHATMA —By L. D. Warren

"NO MORE LET LIFE DIVIDE—WHAT DEATH CAN JOIN TOGETHER"—SHELLEY
—By L. D. Warren

FEEDING THE MOUTH THAT BIT HIM

EVERY MAN TO HIS OWN ENDS!

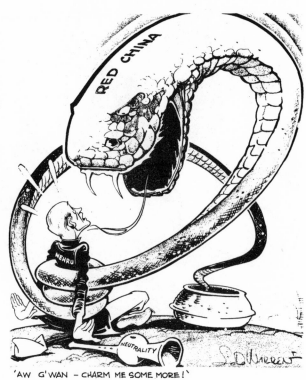

'AW G'WAN – CHARM ME SOME MORE!'

AND THE CALICO CAT REPLIED 'MEE-OW!'

'HONEST, IT ISN'T A TRICK!'

'ANYONE FOR CHICKEN CHOW MEIN?'

FIRE BURN AND CAULDRON BUBBLE

'HOW MANY TIMES DO I HAVE TO WARN YOU KIDS ABOUT PLAYING WITH MATCHES?'

"I CAN'T BUDGE IT - BUT I KNOW WHERE IT'S GOING!"

'YOU HEARD ME! GET OFF! MY FEET ARE KILLING ME!'

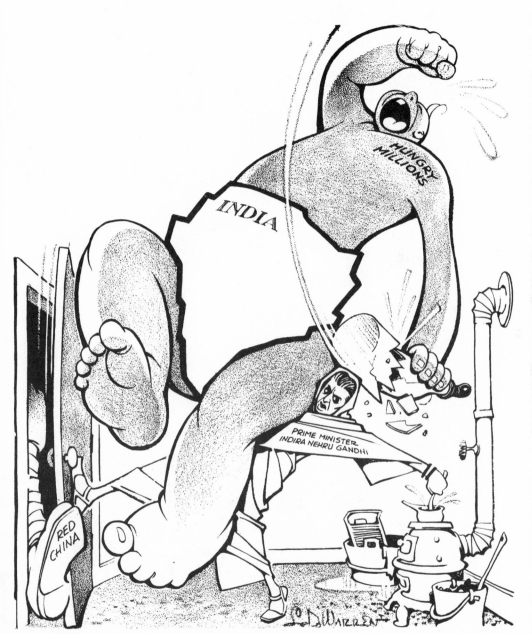

WOMAN'S WORK IS NEVER DONE

'SEEMS TO ME I'VE HEARD THAT SONG BEFORE!'

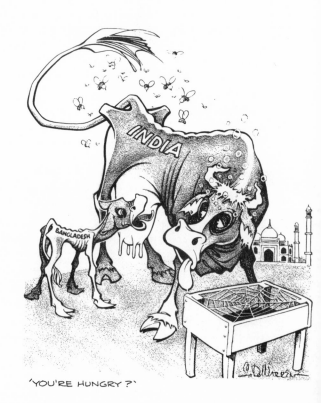

'YOU'RE HUNGRY?'

10

THE TWO CHINAS

The news of the successful Bolshevik Revolution in Russia from 1917 onward exerted a strong influence on many Chinese intellectuals. Already imbued with Western liberal ideas, they readily moved to the Left in thought, and became eager to bring about a similar Communist revolution in their vast and essentially rural country. Moscow gladly assisted their endeavor, and Russian agents were sent to help establish the Chinese Communist party in 1921. Among the native founders of the party was a young library clerk at Peking University named Mao Tse-tung. Mao, born in 1893, was of peasant stock, had a philosophical bent, and early developed strong leadership ability.

During the 1920s, Generalissimo Chiang Kai-shek almost succeeded in destroying the Communists, but Mao survived by collecting a small band of followers and retreating to rugged mountain territory. With infinite patience, he added to his following by appealing specifically to the peasant masses to join him in overthrowing the landlord class. In the 1930s, he evolved a master plan, which he pursued with little variation and much success until he came to power over mainland China in 1949.

The military phase of his plan became the classic formulation of modern guerrilla warfare:

> The enemy advances: we retreat.
> The enemy halts: we harass.
> The enemy tires: we attack.
> The enemy retreats: we pursue.

In the implementation of this strategy, he naturally scored gains and suffered setbacks. Most famous of the latter was a "Long March" that, lasting a year (1934-1935), involved a retreat of 6000 miles with 100,000 men—away from Chiang's southern strongholds to Yennan in the poverty-stricken northern province of Shensi; the survivors numbered barely one-third of the original force.

Between 1937 and 1945, that is, shortly before and during World

War II, Mao was able to make a remarkable comeback, largely because Japanese invaders drained the strength of the ruling Chinese Nationalist party (Kuomintang). By the time of the Japanese surrender to the Allies in 1945, Mao had enlarged the area under his control to include most of the northern countryside. Now, with prompt and extensive Soviet aid, he launched a series of successful surprise attacks and then exerted relentless pressure until, on October 1, 1949, he was able to establish the (Red) People's Republic of China, with its capital in Peking.

Chiang had received considerable American air help in this war, but he and his (sometimes unreliable) generals were no military match for Mao's ever-growing forces—growing, among other reasons, through the wholesale desertion to his side of Nationalist soldiers. In December, 1949, Chiang, with more than a million loyal military and civilian followers, moved the seat of his government to the large island of Taiwan. The United Nations and most Western states recognized this as the legitimate Republic of China, with its capital at Taipei.

The Peking government lost no time in confiscating Western businesses and property and in expelling Western nationals. In order quickly to drive any non-Communist ideas from the minds of the people, and to indoctrinate them with the new ideology and political outlook, small "study groups" were organized in schools, shops, factories, and offices. The "thinking" of the members of each group was reported regularly to the local authorities. Strict censorship, propaganda through all available media, and the imposition of a death penalty for opposition became the order of the day, so that, within less than two years, the Chinese mainland was stamped a fully totalitarian state.

The land was redistributed and peasants were motivated, in emotionally charged meetings, to denounce, and call for the execution of, wicked village landlords. Obviously, no figures are available on the number of landlords killed; but, as a class, the larger-landholding group was liquidated by 1952. Businessmen then also were eliminated as a class. At special meetings, businessmen were "urged" to "confess" their own "capitalistic crimes" and to denounce their competitors. Those who remained alive generally were ready to "share" their enterprises with the state, and, as the 1950s drew to a close, to transfer them to full state control. And many of these were persuaded to demonstrate in public their "joy" at having left capitalism behind.

Red China's chief resource was people, who, by 1973, numbered perhaps 800,000,000, or one-fifth of the world's total. Much of this manpower was inspired to work the land intensively, with sufficient success so that, by the mid-1950s, agricultural "profits" financed industrial development. Through the years, Soviet money, technical assistance, and skilled factory supervision were given to China, and many young Chinese students were sent to study in Russia.

Eventually, however, the prolonged high-pressure tactics and unending demand for almost frenzied activity led to widespread discontent. Accordingly, Mao, in 1957, apparently tried to provide a safety valve by permitting limited criticism of the regime. "Let a hundred flowers bloom," he said, "let a hundred schools contend." But when the relaxation of controls resulted in fewer flowers than in denunciations, the harsh censorship was restored and the dissidents, who thus had made themselves known, were punished severely.

On the other hand, recognizing that much of the discontent stemmed from a drastic shortage of consumer goods, Mao in the same year ordered his countrymen to make a "Great Leap Forward," whereby China would become both a land of plenty and an accepted world power. With Russian advice and equipment, larger plants were constructed in urban areas, and innumerable primitive factories and even backyard furnaces were set up wherever feasible. Simultaneously, farm life was made communal by requiring the peasants to surrender their plots to the state and move to publicly supervised "dormitories."

But the Leap ended in near disaster. One reason was the coincidence in these years of exceptional flooding alternating with ruinous droughts. Another was the fact that the peasants generally disliked the new living arrangements and wanted to return to plots of their own. A third was the shoddy workmanship of the inexperienced factory laborers. Widespread famine in 1960 and 1961, however, conveniently was blamed on the Russians, who had withdrawn most of their technicians and advisers as age-old Sino-Soviet boundary disputes and more recent ideological differences frayed the bonds of friendship.

Many of the rural communes therefore were dissolved and a vigorous, though apparently unsuccessful, campaign was launched to curtail population growth. In 1973, however, it was estimated that the country still had some 70,000 communes, some comprising as many as 15,000 persons each. Gradually, also, blame for China's ills was placed more and more frequently on the United States, which was accused of having "stolen" Taiwan from the Chinese people and of trying through its economic and military might to "enslave" China. In this period, "Protector" Mao's greatest, albeit expensive, triumphs were the detonation of an atomic bomb in 1964 and the launching of an earth-orbiting satellite in 1970.

Meanwhile, a portion of the powerful bureaucracy seemed to have reached the conclusion that Mao was slavishly aping the Soviet pattern and was inept in his approach to economic progress. Apparently, the bureaucrats, especially in the provinces, wanted to destroy the Stalinlike, monolithic political-administrative system that suited the dictator's thinking because it placed him at the apex of the governmental pyramid.

Mao's response to this budding revolution was the organization of millions of teenage "Red Guards," who, in 1966, rioted in the streets, destroyed Buddhist shrines, defamed such traditional heroes as Confucius, and beat and killed an untold number of "reactionaries." By the end of 1967, the Red Guards, through their "Great Proletarian Cultural Revolution," which, in effect, was a civil war, had so disrupted work and life as to bring back famine and industrial breakdown. Thereupon some of the youth were sent back to the schools, factories, and farms.* "Revolutionary Committees," however, continued the purge of anti-Maoist civil and military leaders. In the spring of 1969, Mao officially declared the Cultural Revolution ended, with himself again fully in control.

On the foreign front, Peking, although turned down in 1969 as previously in its application for membership in the United Nations, did resume boundary talks with Moscow and achieved a lessening of trade restrictions on the part of the United States. At last, in 1971, the United Nations, packed with African and Middle Eastern members, did recognize the People's Republic as the "only legitimate representative of China" in the world body. Shortly thereafter, early in 1972, President Nixon visited Red China. The upshot of the visit was a recognition by Washington of Taiwan as "a part of China," the negotiation of a Sino-United States trade agreement, and the granting of tourist visas by each country to nationals of the other. Japan then, also in 1972, recognized Mao's government as the "sole legal government of China," and other countries rapidly followed suit. Tensions thus were lessened—as Red China continued to develop greater nuclear striking power.

Chiang Kai-shek's Taiwan, meanwhile, whose population of less than 13,000,000 in 1965 had risen to more than 15,000,000 in 1972, was a thorn in Mao's side. The latter was much irritated by this nearby open challenge to his might and to the way of life that he extolled. Despite its small size, Taiwan had a relatively large, well-drilled army and had on its soil American air installations and military advisers. In addition, a powerful United States fleet was kept in adjacent waters to forestall an invasion from the mainland. Mao for many years seemed worried lest there be a Nationalist invasion of the mainland, abetted by a strong fifth column of Nationalist sympathizers, spies, and saboteurs.

Beyond this, Taiwan, although firmly ruled by a one-party (Kuomintang) government, adopted wise domestic policies and was a model of economic prosperity and social progress. Most of the Taiwanese peasants owned land, industry developed efficiently with United States help, universal education was a fact not a plan, and the authorities encouraged a sensible program of family planning. So good was the economy, that Taiwan, in 1965, thanked the United States for all its past financial aid

---

*In 1974, the number of university students was estimated at 400,000, or about one of every two thousand inhabitants.

and indicated that it needed no further such subsidy. Taipei, indeed, suggested that other areas stood in far greater need of any further American largesse. In 1972, President Chiang, nearly eighty-five years old, was elected for a sixth five-year term. Obviously, the Nationalist government was upset when Red China generally won recognition as *the* Chinese state; but on the death of Chiang Kai-shek in 1975, his son, Chiang Ching-kuo, remained as premier and Vice President Yen Chia-kan assumed the presidency.

GREEN THUMB?

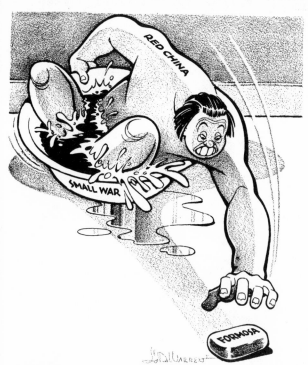

STRETCHING THINGS A BIT TOO FAR

VEST POCKET WAR

YOU CAN'T HARDLY GET THEM NO MORE

'WHEN YOU SIT IN LEFT FIELD _ THEY SOMETIMES LAND RIGHT IN YOUR LAP!'

---THEY JUST FADE AWAY

'YOU KNOW HOW HE HATES WESTERNS!'

'WHO TAUGHT YOU TO DRIVE?'

HIGH YIELDING STRAIN OF WINTER WHEAT

193

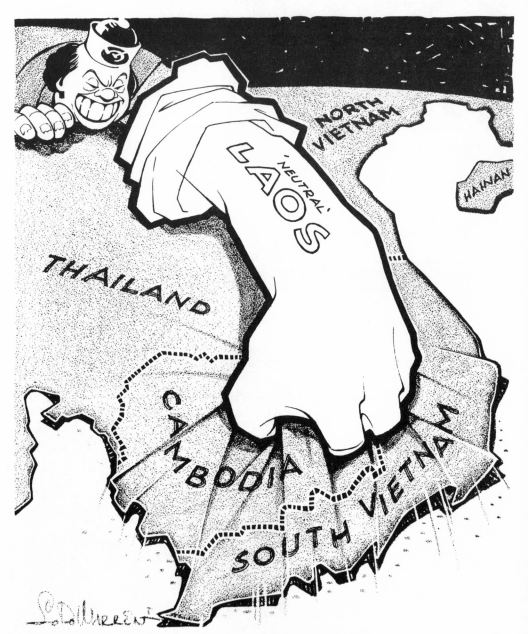

COMMUNIST CONTAINMENT IN SOUTHEAST ASIA

'BUSINESS SEEMS TO BE PICKING UP!'

'ON A SMOGLESS DAY YOU CAN SEE THE REVISIONARY IMPERIALIST SOVIET PIGS!'

11

JAPAN

The occupation of Japan from 1945 onward was a joint Allied obligation. Actual authority, however, was vested in the Supreme Commander for the Allied Forces (SCAP), who initially was the American general, Douglas MacArthur. Inasmuch as it had been decided not to depose Emperor Hirohito (who had ascended the throne in 1926) nor to destroy the basic pattern of Japanese national life, MacArthur issued his directives to and through a largely Japanese-manned administration.

Demilitarization and the trial of "war criminals" proceeded rapidly, for the degree of Japan's military defeat and the fear inspired by nuclear bombing had brought a pacifistic mood to the country. SCAP then moved to "democratize" the empire by presenting to an assembly elected in 1946, an American-drafted constitution. Becoming effective in 1947, this document converted the country into a constitutional monarchy, with a bicameral parliament chosen by universal male and female suffrage. Parliament was given control over the budget and authority to select both premier and cabinet. Civil rights were guaranteed, and Tokyo bound itself never again to make war or to maintain large armed forces. The outstanding native leader until 1954 was Premier Shigeru Yoshida, head of the Liberal Democratic party.

On the economic side, SCAP broke up many of the large family-controlled holding companies, saw to the adoption of the Anti-Monopoly Law (1947), encouraged the formation of trade unions, and inaugurated an ambitious program of land redistribution. Absentee landlordism was prohibited. The merchant marine was rebuilt and enlarged. New industries were created. And wages rose, whereas prices were kept stable.

Education was "democratized," religion and the state were separated, and activities that tended to extol militarism were discouraged. The rapid and fairly smooth process of modernization and Westernization, and the early advent of economic prosperity, offered little grist to the disruptive mill of Communism.

The outbreak of the Korean War and the unease with which the Cold War imbued Americans led President Truman in 1950 to seek an

197

official end to the war with Japan, despite Russia's desire to continue
stalling on Far Eastern peace negotiations. Thereupon, John Foster
Dulles, as Special Ambassador, spent a year visiting ten major capitals
in search of agreement on peace terms. Washington and London eventually agreed on a draft treaty, and fifty-two interested nations were invited
to come to San Francisco in 1951 to sign or reject the completed document.

The treaty in essence was nonpunitive. It restored full sovereignty to
Japan's four main islands and nearby minor islands, and paved the way
for the empire's membership in the United Nations. Trade discrimination
against the former enemy was prohibited. Japan's right to self-defense
measures was recognized. And reparation was limited to payments in
labor and goods.

Most of the invited nations signed the document at the conference, or
soon agreed to separate but similar treaties. Only the Soviet bloc was
adamantine in its refusal, thus technically remaining at war with Japan
as the ensuing decades passed. In Japan, itself, objection was centered
mainly on a bilateral Japanese-United States security agreement that
was signed on the same day as the peace treaty, for this pact permitted
the stationing of United States forces in and around Japan. Practical
considerations prevailed, however, and the treaty became effective in
1952. So Japan regained her sovereign status six years and seven months
after her surrender in World War II. (The last United States ground
forces, ever a target of student and Leftist demonstrations, were withdrawn in 1958.)

The dominant political group in the empire during the quarter-
century after the war was the Liberal Democratic party. It strongly
favored democracy, free enterprise, and a policy friendly to the United
States. Because it came into being through the merger of several like-
minded yet separately led groups, it also began to suffer somewhat from
factionalism, particularly in the late 1960s and the 1970s. Its chief rival,
far behind in popular votes, was the Socialist party. The Communist party,
linked in the public mind with unpopular Russia, made much noise and
created considerable turmoil, but had little political influence.

During the decade from 1964-1974, under Premiers Hayato Ikeda
(1960-1964), Eisaku Sato (1964-1972), and Kakuei Tanaka (1972-
1974), Japan moved steadfastly into the top rank of world industrial
powers. Nipponese manufacturers captured a growing share of the world
market, particularly in such fields as small cars, trucks, and motorcycles.
Parallel with this development, because Japan, also, found itself with
too many people living on too few square miles (and therefore was vul-
nerable to revolutionary propaganda), social and welfare legislation was

sponsored fairly readily even by some of the more conservative parliamentarians.*

In her international relations, Japan, throughout the 1950s and 1960s, aimed at becoming an economically strong bulwark between Communist Asia and the West, especially the United States. Ideology, however, was not allowed to interfere with business, since foreign trade was vital to the well-being of the populace. Japan accordingly negotiated numerous bilateral trade agreements, including some that encouraged the shipment of foreign goods via Japan's large merchant fleet. The oil crisis of 1973-1974, plus the price inflation and growing unemployment that plagued other powers as well, dealt harsh blows to the economy of the empire, and led to increasing unrest in 1974.

Tokyo in 1972 regained from the United States administrative control over Okinawa and full control over Ryukyu, a chain of islands running southward from the large home island of Kyushu to Taiwan. During the same year, a few months after President Nixon had visited Peking and mended Sino-United States relations, Tokyo recognized Peking as the "sole" government of China; trade relations with Taiwan, however, in no way were impaired. Meanwhile, in the early 1970s, *Japan* remained cool to *Soviet* overtures for a peace treaty, as long as Moscow held on to four small Pacific islands, to the north of the empire, that Russia had occupied *after* the end of fighting in World War II.

---

*With her population of 106,000,000 on 145,000 square miles, Japan had twice as many people as France on two-thirds the land area.

WHAT'S IN A NAME!

—By L. D. Warren

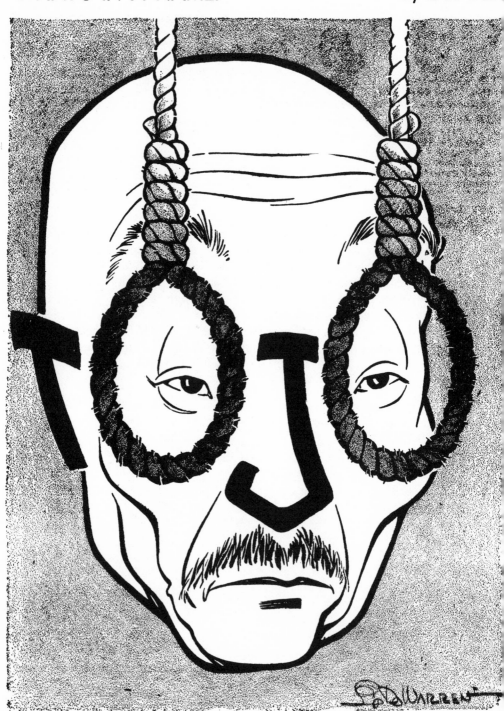

BY ANY OTHER NAME

—By L. D. Warren

MARRING THE JAPANESE SCENE

—By L. D. Warren

—By L. D. Warren

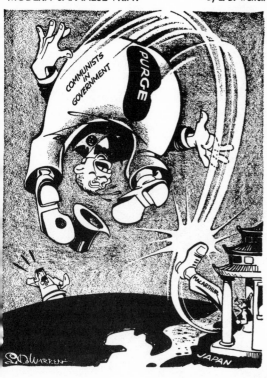

BURIAL '41 AND '51

HATCHED IN AN INCUBATOR

SOMEONE SHOULD GET TO THE JAPANESE SEAT OF LEARNING

'BETTER TO BE THE HEAD OF A CHICKEN THAN THE SOUTH END OF AN OX.' – *EISAKU SATO*

12

AFRICA: WEST, EAST, AND SOUTH

At the close of World War II, all Africa except Egypt, Ethiopia, Liberia, and South Africa still was dominated by European states. Spirits of anticolonialism and of nationalism, however, had emerged in many parts of the continent, and given rise to movements for "liberation" from "imperialism." And within a score of years after 1945, direct European control virtually had been eliminated from Africa—owing in large measure to the leadership of European-educated natives. (By 1974, there were forty-three independent African countries.)

In French West Africa, the disaffection was especially deep because of the authoritarian rule exercised after 1940 by Vichy-oriented French officials. The postwar Paris administration accordingly drafted a constitution that envisaged a federal relationship between the Fourth Republic and French West Africa. When this was rejected by the French electorate, a new draft allotted only 13 of the 622 seats in the Paris National Assembly to West Africans; understandably, this proposal aroused little enthusiasm among the Blacks.

During the early 1950s, the area did experience steady economic and social progress, but unrest persisted, and after the middle of the decade it became obvious to Paris that the natives would be satisfied only with independence. As a first step in this direction, each colony, from 1956 on, was given a measure of internal autonomy. This concession stimulated political activity aimed at achieving further concessions.

De Gaulle, as head of the Fifth Republic, in 1958 offered the Africans membership in the French Community. They would have their own assemblies, under French tutelage, and the right to vote in French presidential elections. Thus the natives might be placated and the French parliament would be spared from a "flood" of African delegates who might convert the mother country into "a colony of her colonies." Although some in the territories seemed to favor the plan, a demand soon arose for outright independence in a loose federation with France. Thereupon de Gaulle, embroiled, as we have seen, in a virtual civil war over Algeria, agreed to independence.

In 1960, then, the eight republics of Mali (formerly the French Sudan), Togo, Cameroon, Mauritania, Niger, Upper Volta, Ivory Coast, and Dahomey were established. They left the French Community and promptly were admitted to membership in the United Nations. Six other colonies also became independent republics in 1960, and joined the UN, but, largely for economic reasons, they remained within the French Community; these were the Central African Republic, Chad, and Gabon (all formerly parts of French Equatorial Africa), Congo-Brazzaville (the erstwhile French Congo), Malagasy (Madagascar), and Senegal.*

All these republics continued to lead precarious existences. They have been disturbed by internal feuds and power struggles among tribal leaders, and are heavily dependent on favorable rains. A number are so small as to be economically unviable and a prey to their imperialistically inclined African neighbors.†

In British West Africa the situation was more complicated. London long had pursued a policy in Nigeria, the Gold Coast and British Togoland (later Ghana), and Sierra Leone of encouraging education, extending social primacy to tribal chiefs, and stimulating the rise of a middle class of journalists, lawyers, and teachers. After 1945, the middle-class professionals in each of these lands rose in revolt, not alone against the British, but against the social system. Leadership in the independence movement in each country was assumed by the abler ones among those natives who had studied abroad; they were aided by many of the soldiers who had fought in World War II in Europe and there had observed at least the outer manifestations of modernization and industrialization. The British colonies also counted among their revolutionaries a number of experienced Communist leaders.

Outstanding among the Gold Coast nationalists was Kwame N. Nkrumah. The British had imprisoned him in 1950 for calling a general strike. While still in jail, he was elected in 1952 to a national assembly, winning largely as a result of the disciplined efforts of the party backing him. Soon after his election, he was released, to become premier in a partly autonomous government. The liberal-minded British governor-general actively supported the prime minister and, by 1954, helped him to bring about direct elections and universal suffrage. Full independence within the Commonwealth was delayed for several years, mainly because of tribal

---

*The French Community also included four Overseas Departments with broad autonomy, and seven Overseas Territories governed by High Commissioners. Only one of the Overseas Territories is in Africa, namely, the Territory of the Afars and the Issas—the former French Somaliland.

†The Belgian Congo in 1960 became the independent Democratic Republic of the Congo. It changed its name in 1971 to Zaïre, with its capital at Kinshasa (Léopoldville).

and other native opposition to Nkrumah. But in 1960, the Gold Coast and British Togoland became the new Republic of Ghana, with Nkrumah as its first president. Flushed with success, he adopted a foreign policy aimed at stimulating independence movements elsewhere in Africa.

Nkrumah's domestic policy was far more repressive than had been that of the British. In addition, he so mismanaged the finances as to bring on virtual bankruptcy; he tolerated widespread corruption and, himself, led a startlingly extravagant life. The army, having grown increasingly restive, ousted him from power in 1966 and set up a military-police state.

Three years later, opportunity was given to an elected parliament and civilian leadership to direct the republic's affairs, but it had little success. There was widespread starvation, tribal tensions became heightened rather than allayed, and the national financial situation became disastrous, in part because of a decline in the world price of cocoa. Once again the army intervened, and in 1972 accepted young Colonel Ignatius K. Acheampong as head of state. The new leader repudiated part of the national debt, sought to achieve a national stance of "self-reliance," and launched an "Operation Reconciliation" to deemphasize tribalism and foster national unity. (He was assassinated early in 1975.)

Nigeria, the most populous country in Africa, with an estimated 73,000,000 inhabitants in 1973, speaking some 250 languages, suffered more than any of its neighbors from tribalism and sectionalism. It became self-governing in 1960 and an independent republic within the Commonwealth in 1963. The constitution provided for a federal state, made up of Northern, Western, and Eastern Nigeria, and, from 1963, a fourth or Midwestern region. As a consequence, popular loyalty generally was regional rather than national, and the country was torn by strife and bloodshed. In an effort to bring relief, Major General Yakubu Gowon assumed dictatorial power in 1966, and during the following year decided to replace the former regions by twelve new states.

The announced reorganization led to the secession in the East of the landlocked and infertile area known as Biafra, inhabited largely by Ibo tribesmen. The resulting cruel war, during which the Ibo were reduced by blockade and starvation to a small fraction of their original number, ended in Biafra's surrender in 1970. The republic's postwar rehabilitation was helped by the discovery and exploitation in Biafra of major oil resources. The resulting oil income reduced the country's dependence on foreign capital and encouraged the government to adopt a policy of "indigenization," particularly in the service industries. Both foreign management and foreign labor gradually were replaced by Nigerian personnel. A tentative date of 1976 was set for return from military to civilian government.

East Africa was largely under British control before World War II. It was made up essentially of Kenya, Uganda, and Tanganyika (called Tanzania after its union in 1964 with the nearby islands of Zanzibar and Pemba). In Kenya, the reaction after 1945 of the estimated 5,000,000 natives against the resident 20,000 Europeans and 120,000 Asians was especially severe. There the Western missionaries for scores of years bitterly had attacked the local tribal customs and societal patterns. Thousands of Kenyans, moreover, had fought in World War II and experienced contact with Western ways and outlooks. Postwar economic dislocation combined with rapid population growth created general hardship. And in 1946 there came to Nairobi from rural Kenya the imposing nationalist leader of the Kikuyu tribe, Jomo (Burning Spear) Kenyatta.

Kenyatta promptly organized the Kenya African National Union (KANU), whose striking arm was the secret Mau Mau society, composed mainly of war veterans. Although he himself opposed the terrorism and depredations of the Mau Mau, the gruesome attacks on European farms continued until Great Britain, in 1952, declared a state of emergency and flew in British troops. Kenyatta was imprisoned and, by 1960, most of the Mau Mau had been killed and many Kikuyu tribesmen forced back from the Nairobi area to their already overcrowded and arid rural villages. Tribal rivalries now soon became political rivalries, particularly between the Kikuyu and the Luo. Yet, in 1963, Kenya received self-government and in 1964 became an independent republic with a unicameral parliament. Kenyatta at once was chosen president. In 1970, aged close to eighty, he began another five-year term.

Kenyatta's prestige and intelligence enabled him to provide a relatively stable government and to keep the continuing tribal disputes from leading to outright civil war. The country is poor in natural resources but possesses magnificent scenery, so that it has remained largely agricultural while developing a lucrative tourist industry. By 1973, the population was estimated at more than 12,000,000, and considerable progress had been made in the (usually forced) "Kenyanization" of economic activity. The landholdings of the Whites were confiscated, and the Asian Indians, who controlled most of the urban business enterprises, lived in constant fear of dispossession and expulsion. A treaty of 1967 created a loose East African community consisting of Kenya, Tanzania, and Uganda. But Kenyatta's hopes for strong regional development were frustrated by serious differences between the leaders of the other two neighboring states.

Tanganyika, once a German colony, became a republic within the Commonwealth in 1962. The march toward independence was led by President Julius K. Nyerere who, in 1964, persuaded the offshore Republic of Zanzibar and Pemba to join Tanganyika as the United Republic of Tanzania. Nyerere was reelected in 1965 and again in 1970, and under his leadership the country moved toward "African Socialism." There were the usual problems facing new African nations, including tribal disputes and a population "explosion" that almost tripled the number of inhabitants (to some 14,000,000) in thirty years. In addition, Nyerere had difficulty persuading semiautonomous Zanzibar to coordinate its Communist-tinged policies with his Socialistic ones, and in keeping his borders intact against Ugandan invasions.

The nationalist movement in land-locked Uganda was held back after 1945, not by the British administrators, but by tradition-minded tribal chiefs who wished to retain their influence within the existing system. By 1960, however, Apollo Milton Mobote brought together a coalition of pro-independence groups, which found the British ready to negotiate. Self-government was achieved in 1962, with Mobote as prime minister; four years later he became president of a federated republic, whose largest element was the kingdom of Buganda.

The political arrangement did not work well, and, since Mobote in any case favored centralization, he issued a constitution, in 1967, which eliminated the kingdom and placed full national power in his hands. He soon announced a program of "Ugandan Socialism," and thereafter displayed some skill in playing off Western and Communist "friends" against one another. But economic progress was slow in this country with few natural resources save scenery, and with a fifth of its area made up of water and swampland. Yet population again grew rapidly, and by 1973 was estimated at 11,000,000.

In 1971, Mobote was ousted by General Idi Amin Dada, who as president continued the dictatorial system, but functioned by impulse and in somewhat erratic fashion. He praised Adolf Hitler for the latter's anti-Semitic policies, without warning took over foreign property, and frequently ordered military violations of the Tanzanian border. In 1972, he expelled some 54,000 of the perhaps 75,000 Asian Indian inhabitants. More than half of these penniless victims, who generally held British passports, were given emergency air transportation to England, the rest gonig to the United States, Canada, and India.

Ethiopia, under French-educated and Christian Emperor Haile Selassie (born in 1892), experienced little change for nearly thirty years after World War II. Since the country already was independent, the drive for modernization lacked the additional stimulus of anticolonialism and was slower in making itself felt than in other parts of Africa. The 27,000,000 inhabitants (1973 estimate) spoke some seventy languages and several hundred dialects, and were divided religiously into Coptic Christians, Moslems, and pagans.

A new constitution and some political reform were promulgated in 1955, a succession of five-year plans for economic development was launched, several harbors were built along the Red Sea, and the country's first university was opened in 1962. Haile Selassie maintained a friendly attitude toward the United States, simultaneously playing a leadership

role in a search for African unity on matters of general concern. Much
to his regret, the move toward unity among the scores of new countries,
with their disparate and sometimes conflicting aims and ambitions, was
evident more in words than deeds.

The pace of Ethiopia's liberalization and modernization was too slow
to satisfy some of the younger military and civilian leaders. These took
the opportunity provided by a 1960 visit of the emperor to Brazil to
attempt a coup d'état and put the crown prince on the throne. Haile
Selassie returned at once and, with the help of loyal army and air force
contingents, defeated the rebels. In the late 1960s and early 1970s, however, rebellion was successful, for this time it involved not only military
and civilian officials, but radical students and the Moslem Arabian population of recently annexed Eritrea.

During World War II, British forces helped Haile Selassie drive out the
Italian Fascists who, under the pretext of performing a "civilizing mis-
sion," had conquered his empire in 1935-1936. After the war, the United
Nations agreed to Haile Selassie's request for the federation of the
former Italian colony of Eritrea on the Red Sea with Ethiopia, thus giving
Addis Ababa direct access to the sea. Then, in 1962, ten years after
federation was achieved, the oligarchic Eritrean assembly voted to give
up the area's autonomous status and Eritrea became a province of
Ethiopia.

Before long, some of the Moslem Arabs in Eritrea founded a
separatist movement and demanded independence. The nationalist movement grew slowly at first, but was helped by the undisciplined behavior
of the Ethiopian troops sent to control the province. Virtual civil war
dragged on for more than a decade and added materially to the still
existing disaffection among military and political leaders in Addis Ababa
as well as among emerging radical student leaders. In 1974, then, the
army toppled Haile Selassie from the throne, executed officials still loyal
to him, and sought to rule through a system of committees—this even
after the abolition of the monarchy in 1975. Not unexpectedly, the
committee system and the absence of a single strong leader stimulated
factionalism and turmoil, encouraged further rebellion in Eritrea, and cast
a deep shadow over the fortune of the empire which, according to Ethiopian tradition, was founded about 1000 B.C. by Menelik I, son of King
Solomon and the Queen of Sheba.

South Africa was unique among African nations after World War I.
There, White control was exercised not by a European colonial power,
but by the descendants of Netherlands settlers (the first of whom came to
the Cape Town area in 1652); of French, German, and Scandinavian
settlers who started coming soon thereafter; and of Britishers who
started immigrating in 1820. The residents of Netherlands's descent
usually have been called Boers, meaning farmers; since the eighteenth

century, all the non-British Whites have been known as Afrikaners (speaking Afrikaans), as distinct from the Black Africans. In this part of Africa, therefore, Black nationalism came to be confronted by a native White nationalism.

The estimated total population in 1973 was more than 24,000,000. Of these, some 4,000,000 were White, 18,000,000 were Black, 2,000,000 were "Colored" or Mixed, and 650,000 were Asians, largely Indian. The Afrikaners, comprising about 60 percent of the White total, have tended to be the conservative element in the political, social, and racial spheres. The remaining 40 percent, of British background, have tended to be the liberal element and have been prominent in the industrial sector of the economy. The dominant Black group, collectively known as Bantus, numbered approximately 14,000,000, and used nearly a hundred different languages; their direct ancestors, driven southward by more warlike Black expansionists from the north, arrived in the region of South Africa later than did the early European settlers.

After World War II, at least three ways to deal with the racial dilemma were open to the government. One choice was the establishment of a political and social order with no discrimination. Another, was the absolute separation of Whites and Blacks in an "apartheid" society. Between these two, was the possibility of creating White and Black communities, living side by side, but with the recognition of differences between them.

The all-White parliament, dominated from 1948 on by the National party and motivated in part by the fear common to minorities surrounded by a different-thinking majority, chose the alternative of apartheid. Beginning in 1949, laws were adopted that officially classified all inhabitants by race, forbade sexual relations between Whites and non-Whites, reserved certain employment categories to Whites, restricted the living quarters of Black urban workers to the outskirts of the cities, established White and Black labor unions, forbade Blacks to strike, excluded Blacks from White places of recreation and entertainment, and the like.

The Bantu Authorities Act of 1951, outlined the eventual creation of semiautonomous Black provinces or tribal homelands called Bantustans. The first such territory, with considerable home rule, was Transkei, created in 1963, and inhabited by some 4,000,000 members of the Xhosa tribe. By 1974, there were eight such Bantustans, and in each there was a growing demand for independence.

The stern enforcement of apartheid led to much violence. British official and public disapproval of the policies led South Africa to leave the Commonwealth in 1961, and to become the Republic of South Africa. The former German colony of South West Africa, which had become a League of Nations mandate after World War I, was virtually incorporated into the republic and made subject to the same legislation. South Africa kept its hold over the area even after the United Nations protested the action. From 1966, the United Nations regarded South West Africa as the new state of Namibia, but to this South Africa paid no attention. A United Nations embargo on economic relations with South Africa was observed by some members, but disregarded, in whole or in part, by others.* The embargo, indeed, was disregarded quietly even by some of the Black African states.

External pressure seemed chiefly to harden the apartheid attitude, at least until the early 1970s. The republic, rich in gold and other minerals, strove to achieve not alone military strength but a considerable measure of economic self-sufficiency. Its strong anti-Communist stance, its attractiveness as a field for foreign investment, and its geographic location on the sea route between the West and Asia—especially after President Nasser in 1956 nationalized the Suez Canal, all made it an important strategic bulwark between the West and the Reds in Africa and Asia.

Eventually, as the older citizens gave way to younger ones in positions of authority, the restrictions of apartheid in the larger cities began to be eased, first in sports, then in the theater, and later in parks, libraries, art galleries, and so forth. Premier Balthazar Johannes Vorster, who came to office in 1966 as a devoted advocate of apartheid, gradually agreed to a lessening of discrimination. After Portugal, in 1974, made ready to give independence to her colonies in southern Africa, Vorster opened dialogues with the heads of several Black African states.†

---

*The United States for some years forbade the importation of chrome ore from South Africa, but permitted the purchase of the same South African ore from Russia at a much higher price.

†In 1971, the author attended services in the Episcopal St. Mary's Church in Johannesburg, at which several of the communion ministrants, a portion of the choir, and nearly a third of the pew occupants were Black.

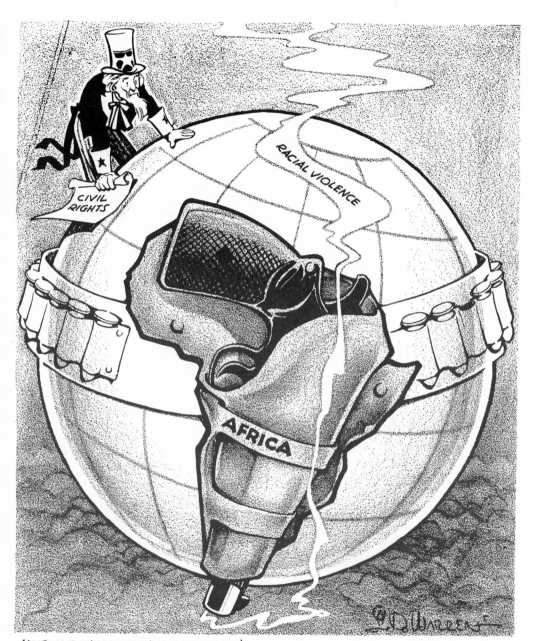

'AND WE THINK WE HAVE A PROBLEM'

'I'M BEGINNING TO WORRY — THEY ACT MORE LIKE PEOPLE EVERY DAY!'

'MAO! WHAT KIND OF GAS HAVE YOU BEEN USING?'

'STOP! WHAT ARE YOU TRYING TO DO? CHOKE HIM TO DEATH?'

SOME SANTAS DO NOT BELIEVE IN CHRISTMAS

MORE TO BE DESIRED THAN GOLD

THEIRS NOT TO REASON WHY - - -

FATHER'S WORK IS NEVER DONE

—By L. D. Warren

'YOU REMEMBER ME! ANDROCLES! I PULLED THAT THORN OUT OF YOUR PAW!'

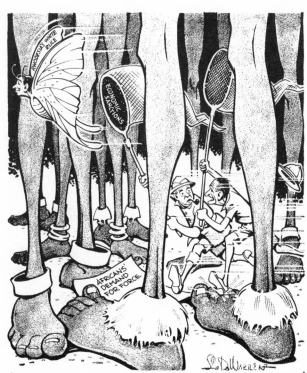

'GREAT EXERCISE, HAROLD — BUT WE'RE STEPPING ON THE TOES OF MY FRIENDS!'

'I DON'T CARE WHAT THE LION SAID! YOU ARE WHITE....WITH BLACK STRIPES!'

'I STILL THINK YOU'RE UGLY! GET LOST!'

SANCTIONS AGAINST RHODESIA

'COME ON IN-THE WATER'S FINE!'

'I'LL GIVE YOU ONE MORE CHANCE! GIVE UP?'

'DON'T BE SURPRISED IF THIS HURTS YOU MORE THAN IT DOES ME!'

'I CAUGHT HIM DEMONSTRATING FOR HIS RIGHTS IN AFRICA, YOUR HONOR!'

13

LATIN AMERICA

The development of Latin America after 1945 was characterized by continuing unrest. The root causes of the troubles were many. Widespread poverty and economic insecurity were compounded by rapidly expanding populations. The growing urbanization of the peasantry was accompanied by a loosening of the hold of the Roman Catholic church over the masses. Governmental instability was reflected in violence perpetrated by extremists of both the Right and the Left. And there was frustration growing out of an admitted need for help from the traditionally disliked "Yankee imperialists."

Covering some 7,700,000 square miles, Latin America, in 1974, was estimated to have about 275,000,000 inhabitants. Approximately 10 percent of the area was in tillage. The mountainous regions often were rich in natural resources, but, except for oil and some metals, these generally were untapped even in the early 1970s. Illiteracy ranged from perhaps 10 percent in Argentina to more than 80 percent in Haiti.

New prestige came with membership in the United Nations. Here the Latin-American group, usually represented by able delegates, gradually became a powerful force in cooperation with the Afro-Asian bloc. With United States sponsorship, there was formed, in 1948, the Organization of American States (OAS). This, in effect, was a defensive alliance system against potential non-American aggressors, and it bound its members to settle their own disputes peaceably. In 1961, on the initiative of President Kennedy, there was formed the Alliance for Progress. This called for a cooperative effort on the part of the American states, except Communist Cuba, to stimulate economic prosperity and "social mobility" through self-help bolstered by financial and technical aid from the United States.

This "grand design" encountered numerous roadblocks. Chief among them, perhaps, were the shortage of economic expertise in Latin America and the prevailing governmental instability. For a time, in the late 1950s, it appeared that the emergence of an enlightened middle class might put an end to the game of "musical chairs" played by successive dictators.

But the still weak social and economic base of most of the republics led to a revival of authoritarian rule in the mid-1960s.

The economic and political climate of Latin America was favorable to the growth of national Communist parties. These lustily attacked the United States and called, first, for nonalignment, and eventually for a pro-Soviet or even a pro-Maoist posture in international affairs. Indeed, it was with practical encouragement from Moscow that the first success-ful Communist takeover occurred, namely, that in Cuba in 1959.

There, ninety miles from Florida, the Communists, led by the thirty-two-year-old guerrilla leader Dr. Fidel Castro Ruíz, overthrew the dicta-torship of General Fulgencio Batista—and substituted a Red dictatorship. In 1960, Castro confiscated all United States property on the island and, early in 1961, Washington severed diplomatic relations with Havana. An American-trained, Florida-based group of Cuban refugees in April, 1961, attempted an invasion in the area of the Bay of Pigs (Bahia de Cochinos). President Kennedy assumed responsibility for the poorly planned and ill-fated venture, and the United States was denounced afresh by the world-wide Red communications media as a vicious aggressor.

Castro now rapidly increased his reliance on Soviet supplies, techni-cians, and advisers, and, in 1962, permitted the construction of Russian offensive missile bases on Cuban soil. When this activity was detected in October by high-flying American reconnaissance planes, President Ken-nedy took so firm a stand that Moscow ordered the return of a fleet of missile-carrying vessels en route to the island. When Washington then promised not to invade Cuba, the Russians agreed to dismantle and remove the existing missile installations.

Most of the Latin-American states thereafter, and until the early 1970s, ostracized Cuba, being all the readier to do so because of Castro's efforts to export *Fidelismo*. Cuban-trained guerrillas were sent throughout South and Central America to organize national Communist takeovers. The ablest such organizer was Castro's chief aide, the Argentine-born Ernesto "Che" Guevara; he was killed in 1967 while trying to stimulate a revolution in Bolivia. Internally, Cuba continued to suffer from its basic dependence on the single crop of sugar; from the loss of about 500,00 exiles, among them many of the best-educated and skilled citizens of the republic; and from the continuing state of political, economic, and moral isolation.

The one Latin-American country that never broke relations with Cuba was Mexico. This federal republic, with an estimated population of 52,000,000 (1974), functioned under a Socialist constitution adopted in 1917. It continued for decade after decade to face virtually the same difficulties and same discontents. President Luis Echeverria Álvarez, elected for a six-year term in 1970, was as occupied as were his pred-

ecessors with the demands of economic nationalism in a large developing country.

The pace of agrarian and labor reform still left the republic suffering
from widespread poverty. The numerous and often isolated rural areas
continued to lack adequate educational facilities, and the urban centers
were plagued by the usual problems of overpopulation. The available
natural resources remained underdeveloped. The "Mexicanization" of
foreign business made difficult the procuring of much-needed foreign
capital. Internal communication and transportation were improved, particularly to sites lucrative as tourist attractions, but there remained need
of more and better roads. Violent outbursts by students and other young
radicals, such as the attempt to disrupt the Mexican Olympic Games in
1968, were not infrequent.

Discontent, frustration, and violence also were characteristic of life
in the postwar decades in Argentina, with its estimated population of
25,000,000 (1974). A mixed national-socialist militarism brought Fas-
cist General Juan Domingo Perón into prominence during a revolt in
1943; three years later he became president. Until his overthrow by the
military in 1955, Perón, with the backing of the army and labor, and
with the benefit of a popular adoration of his young blonde wife Eva,
used censorship and force as his chief instruments for seeking to make
of the republic a Great Power. His demagogic pursuit of economic nationalism and anti-Yankeeism, and his radical social-welfare dictates, ran the
country deeply into debt and confusion.

After his ouster by military conservatives and his exile in Spain,
Perónism continued as a disruptive element in Argentina's political life
through a period of alternating military (anti-Communist) and civilian
administrations. Most of these governments functioned dictatorially and
were hampered by a chronically bad economy, severe inflation (64
percent in 1972 alone), and Rightist-Leftist feuds among labor and other
Perónistas who, despite their violent internecine disagreements, continued
to be "the country's largest and liveliest political force."

In November-December, 1972, the seventy-seven-year-old Perón was
permitted to visit Argentina. He and the then president of the junta and
the republic, Lieutenant General Alejandro Agustín Lanusse, hoped that
the mellowed ex-leader might be able to reconcile his followers and
restore quiet. Perón also hoped that unity in a coalition might enable
his splintered followers to elect a president in 1973, preferably his local
representative, Dr. Héctor J. Cámpora, a dentist. Meanwhile, after the
death of Perón's first wife in Spain, he had married another young blonde
woman, a former cabaret dancer named Maria Estella (Isabelita) Mar-
tínez; she accompanied him on his visit.

Cámpora did win the presidency in 1973, but resigned after fifty days in office so as to pave the way for a return of Perón. The Peróns were allowed to come back in June, 1973, and in September, the former dictator was elected by 62 percent of the votes cast, the largest majority in Argentina's presidential history. And Mrs. Perón was elected vice president. In the next year, 1974, Perón died, and his widow became president.

Although Leftist labor apparently had not given strong support in the election to the Peróns, they proceeded to decree large pay increases for workers, to lower taxes on food staples and wine, and to promote construction of new public works. The importation of many goods was restricted, and a credit of more than a billion dollars was extended to Cuba to stimulate Argentine production. But economic distress, inflation, turmoil, a shortage of foreign capital to develop oil and other natural resources, and border disputes with Chile and Uruguay continued to make life difficult in the unhappy republic.

Largest by far, in area and population, of any Latin-American state, was the Federal Republic of Brazil. Its area of nearly 3,300,000 square miles contained an estimated population, in 1974, of 101,000,000. From 1930-1945, Brazil was under the dictatorship of President Getulio Dornelles Vargas, who joined the Allies in World War II. His political authoritarianism and rigid economic planning displeased many upper-class and professional leaders, whereas the masses, whom he favored in his programs, were irate because of the wartime rise of prices and shortage of consumer goods.

After having been ousted by the military in 1945, he was reelected president for five years in 1950, largely because he had courted success-fully the backing of labor. During the interval between his terms, many of his earlier decrees regulating industry and agriculture had been re-scinded, and social mobility had been fostered. But these and other efforts to stimulate free enterprise had not produced the prosperity that their advocates had promised. Hence a return to strict governmental regulation, already under way when Vargas regained power, was accelerated by him and his cabinet. Except for some increase in the production of capital goods, the results were disappointing. Frustrated, tired, and blamed for the attempted assassination of an opposition newsman, Vargas ended his life in 1954.

Elections of 1955 brought to the presidency the grandson of a Czech immigrant, Juscelino Kubitschek de Oliveira. He quickly launched an unprecedentedly ambitious economic program, hoping to bring "fifty years' progress in five." Among other measures, he moved (1960) the nation's capital to the new and still unfinished city of Brasilia, nearly 600 miles northwest of Río de Janeiro. The removal was intended to lessen the hold of the "establishment" in Río on the national administration, and to encourage the rising generations to leave the crowded coastland and find satisfaction and prosperity in developing the thinly-populated but potentially rich hinterland.

Kubitschek also urged well-to-do Brazilians to invest in home industries, worked hard to attract foreign capital, and put public funds into new enterprises when private money offerings were inadequate. Unhappily, the rapid infusion of investment cash, coupled with inexperience, led to corruption, to a threefold rise in the cost of living between 1955 and 1960, and, eventually, to widespread industrial unemployment.

During the decade of the 1960s, none of several presidents completed a full term in office and none was able to bring prosperity or maintain order. There were alternating periods of Leftist and Rightist influence, increasing demagoguery, growing official corruption, continuing propagandistic attacks on the United States, too-rapid population expansion in the urban areas, various threats of industrial nationalization, and extensive unrest. There was some positive development in the spheres of health, education, and transportation.

In October, 1969, the National Congress, dominated by the conservative National Renovating Alliance (ARENA), chose General (ret.) Emilio G. Médici as president. At the end of his five-year term, in 1974, the electoral college, made up of conservative members of the national and state legislatures, by prearrangement picked General Ernesto Geisel, a former director of the state oil monopoly, as his successor. The military leadership was authoritarian and restrictive of civil liberty; but through careful economic planning by civilian experts, the intelligent exploitation of natural resources, sensible modification of the tax structure, corrective action where bureaucratic corruption or inefficiency were involved, improved relations with the Roman Catholic church, and the encouragement of foreign tourism, it brought to the republic an almost spectacular economic improvement and a position of greater prestige in international affairs.

DIPLOMATIC DILEMMA

TO TANGO IT ALWAYS TAKES TWO

'THOU SHALT HAVE NO OTHER GODS BEFORE FIDEL!'

THE PIED PIPER OF HAVANA

'HALT! WHO GOES THERE?'

WHEN SMALL MEN CAST LONG SHADOWS _ THE SUN IS SETTING!

ANOTHER BIG BLOW IN THE CARIBBEAN

'NOW ALL WE HAVE TO DO IS INVITE A FEW INNOCENT LONELY FLIES!'

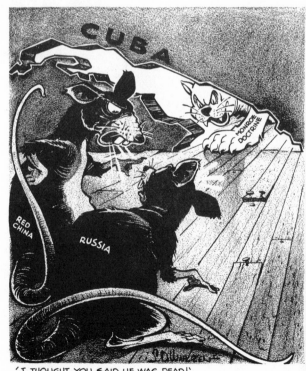

'I THOUGHT YOU SAID HE WAS DEAD!'

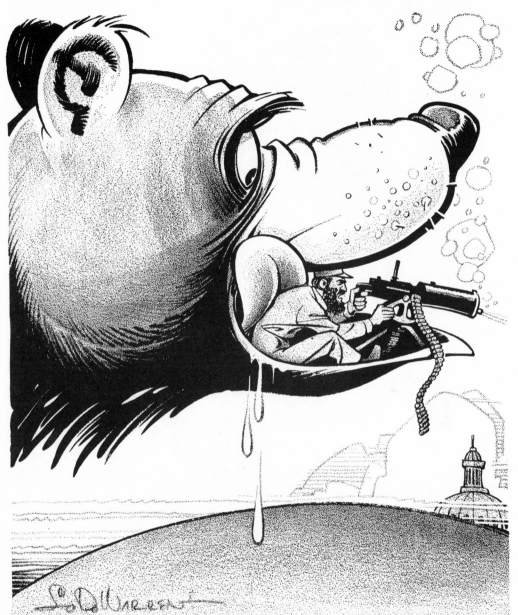

'THE FREEDOM-loving CUBAN PEOPLE MUST BE PROTECTED FROM U.S. AGGRESSION'-USSR

'IT'S LATER THAN YOU THINK!'

'IT CAN'T BE WHAT I THINK IT IS BECAUSE WE HAVE AN AGREEMENT THAT THEY WON'T DO WHAT I THINK THEY'RE DOING!'

'YOUR BIGGEST MISTAKE, FIDEL — WAS IN ADMITTING YOU WERE A COMMUNIST!'

"SHAKE-RATTLE AND ROLL!!"

WAITING FOR THE DUST TO SETTLE!

"NOW YOU KEEP OUT OF THIS!"

'ARISE! DANCE FOR ME!'

'WHAT DOES THE PAPER HAVE TO SAY ABOUT PRESIDENT NIXON'S NEW POLICY?'

WHEN THE BOUGH BREAKS---

U.S. AGREES TO REVISE CANAL ZONE TREATIES

14

THE UNITED STATES

Upon the death of Franklin D. Roosevelt, in April, 1945, Vice President Harry S Truman succeeded to the presidency of the United States.* Although on occasion displaying pettiness and an exaggerated loyalty to friends even when these were corrupt, Truman worked hard to learn the intricacies of governmental operation and soon showed himself capable of making and sticking to decisions. By the time of the election of 1948, he had persuaded Congress to establish a presidential Council of Economic Advisers, to place control over nuclear power in the hands of the civilian Atomic Energy Commission rather than the military, to bring all the armed services under the civilian head of a new Department of Defense, and to support his economic (Marshall Plan) and political strategy (Truman Doctrine) in the Cold War.

To the astonishment of many experienced political observers, and of the Republican party, Truman in 1948 defeated his Republican opponent for the presidency, Thomas E. Dewey of New York—who himself had been so sure of victory as not to exert himself unduly during the campaign. In 1949, then, Truman launched a liberal domestic program, which he christened the "Fair Deal" in follow-up of Roosevelt's "New Deal." But despite a Democratic majority in Congress, Truman generally was unable to get his proposals enacted because of an opposition coalition of Republicans and Southern Democrats.

The Truman administration also was plagued by evidence of corruption in high places and by a "Red Scare" based originally on the discovery of Communist spying in government offices. Largely through the energetic efforts of Congressman Richard M. Nixon, who was a member of the House Committee on Un-American Activities, a former senior officer in the Department of State named Alger Hiss was convicted in 1949 of having headed an anti-United States spy ring. During the next year, the Federal Bureau of Investigation accused Julius and Ethel Rosenberg of having passed atomic secrets to Russia. In 1953, after a prolonged trial, the convicted couple was executed.

---

*President Truman did not use a period after the initial S.

Senator Joseph McCarthy of Wisconsin, apparently impressed by the prominence that came to Nixon for his anti-Communist work, in 1949 started a headline-producing campaign of his own against the Department of State—eventually even implying that President Dwight D. Eisenhower was the victim of Red influence. Thereafter McCarthy's tactics fell into disrepute. Discredited and censured by his colleagues in the Senate, he died in relative obscurity in 1957. Gradually, a sizable segment of the public had become convinced that the external threat of Communism, as manifested in the Cold War, was more dangerous to the United States than any internal threat.

Meanwhile, Truman's already waning popularity had suffered further decline when, in 1951, he recalled the popular war-hero, General Douglas MacArthur, from his post as commander of the United Nations Forces in the Korean War and as head of the Allied Command in Japan. Whereas Administration policy was to fight a "limited war," MacArthur, despite official notice not to do so, publicly urged the extension of military operations beyond Korea to China—which was helping Red-controlled North Korea. Deciding then that the issue of civilian control over the military was at stake, the president recalled MacArthur. The latter returned to a hero's welcome and accepted an invitation to address a joint session of Congress. Truman thereupon decided not to run for reelection in 1952.

The Democrats now nominated Governor Adlai E. Stevenson of Illinois, who faced General Eisenhower on the Republican ticket. "Ike," as he soon came to be called by the communications media, won a sweeping personal victory, running well ahead of his party's vote for Congress. The popularity of the new president—an unpretentious man of moderate views, who was more interested in what seemed to him good for the country than good for any political faction—increased during the passing years, and in 1956 he again defeated Stevenson. But the Democrats gained control of both Houses.

Shortly after his first election, Eisenhower kept a campaign promise to visit Korea. Having made it plain to the Chinese and Russians that the war must be permitted to come to an early end or else would be fought over a larger area, he won Communist acquiescence to an agreement that eventually ended the fighting in July, 1953.

Although his political opponents, especially those among the "liberal" intellectuals, belittled President Eisenhower's ability and achievements, his administration successfully fostered significant legislation. The Social Security System was expanded. The Civil Rights Act of 1957 was adopted to protect the voting rights of Black Americans. In order to help retrieve the technological leadership apparently lost when the Soviet Union launched the satellite Sputnik I, in 1957, the National Defense Education Act of 1958 provided federal support for research and instruction in science, mathematics, and languages. And the Labor-Management Reporting and Disclosure Act of 1959 was aimed at reducing racketeering and other abuses that had found their way into labor-union practices.

The election of 1960 pitted Vice President Nixon against Democratic candidate John F. Kennedy, a Roman Catholic senator from Massachusetts. Nixon's agreement to debate the issues over television reacted in favor of the youthful Kennedy, who until then had had by far the less national exposure, and whose "charisma" was shown to good advantage. The election was close, with Kennedy polling only 113,000 more votes than Nixon, out of nearly 69,000,000 votes cast.

Kennedy's "New Frontier" program had virtually no success in Congress, again because the president could not dent the opposition of Southern Democrats and Republicans. In foreign affairs there was more activity. For the first time, thousands of troops were sent to Vietnam. The Cold War almost became hot in 1962 before Russia, under threat of war, withdrew nuclear-missile equipment secretly sent to Cuba and reversed the course of a Soviet fleet of missile-carrying ships en route to Fidel Castro's island. And the economic Alliance for Progress was formed with Latin America.

Then, on November 22, 1963, to the horror of much of the world, the president was shot and killed in Dallas. Within ninety-eight minutes of the victim's death, Vice President Lyndon B. Johnson of Texas was sworn in as chief executive.

Johnson's political "savvy" and long experience in Congress enabled him to get approval for much of his "Great Society" program, aimed at lessening poverty by providing education and practical training to the poor. This success led the Republican leaders to believe that they would not win in 1964 unless they could oppose to the renominated Johnson a man who would offer the voters "a choice not an echo." The mantle was placed on the conservative Senator Barry Goldwater of Arizona.

The campaign was marked by "mud-slinging" and some rash utterances by Goldwater, who relied for guidance on a corps of inexperienced advisers. Johnson won by the largest spread of votes in the country's history, gaining much support, on the one hand, because of Goldwater's repudiation of social-welfare and civil-rights legislation, and, on the other, because of the Arizonian's advocacy of a quick end to the Vietnamese involvement by whatever force might be needed.

During Johnson's first full term, the legislature enacted most of his domestic recommendations, adopting heavily funded measures to alleviate poverty in Appalachia and for urban, especially Black, aid. Additional laws allocated large sums to subsidize college students and improve the offerings of public schools. Despite all this, Johnson's popularity plummeted as heavy rioting marred life in Northern cities and United States involvement in Southeast Asia became ever deeper.

Four-score years after Abraham Lincoln's death, Black Americans still were segregated and widely discriminated against in education, employment, housing, organized sports, the armed services, and voting rights. But with the backing of Presidents Truman, Eisenhower, Kennedy, Johnson, and Nixon, gradual improvement occurred in the decades after World War II.

The nation's first fair-employment practices act was adopted in 1945, in New York State. The "color line" in professional sports was broken when Jackie R. Robinson joined the Brooklyn Dodgers baseball team in 1947. Dr. Ralph J. Bunche, grandson of a slave, was appointed to high posts in the Department of State and the United Nations, and, in 1950, received the Nobel Peace Prize for his skill in mediating an Arab-Israeli dispute some years earlier. Integration of the armed forces came about during the Korean War.

In 1954, the Supreme Court reversed an earlier decision by ruling that "separate education facilities are inherently unequal." In 1955, the Court ordered desegregation of all school districts. For a time, the Court's orders were defied, particularly in the Deep South. Indeed, in 1957, President Eisenhower used federal troops to assure the entry of some Black students to Central High School in Little Rock, Arkansas. And in 1962, protected by hundreds of United States marshals, James Meredith became the first Black student to be enrolled at the University of Mississippi.

Meanwhile, a highly articulate young Black minister, the Reverend Martin Luther King, Jr., with support from Washington, had won battles in Montgomery, Alabama, for the desegregation of buses, and in Birmingham for the opening of public facilities to all Americans. By the time Congress, in 1964, provided for the withholding of federal funds from any project receiving federal money if discrimination were proved, King had become prominent as the outstanding Black civil-rights leader.

Meanwhile, also, the center of Black dissatisfaction had moved northward, particularly to the industrial areas that soon after World War I had begun to attract large-scale Black migration from the South. More often than not, those who had come in hope of a good life, found themselves no less poor than before, barred from the higher-paid jobs, and living in Black "ghettos" at exorbitant rentals. Thus the Black problem was added to the many other problems of crowded and smoky urban centers. The march toward political civil rights meant little to the Blacks as long as their ghetto walls were upheld by economic restrictions.

The long-continued frustrations now sometimes were fired into violence by militant Black power-seeking leaders and by White radicals who saw in Black discontent an opportunity for overturning society. From 1964, urban areas began to experience major riots, arson, pillaging, wholesale looting, and attacks on policemen, firemen, and National Guardsmen—all this frequently and tragically in the already poor sections of the cities. And then, in 1968, Dr. King, who had not endorsed the tactics of the "Black Power" advocates, was assassinated in Memphis, Tennessee. This traumatic experience for the nation, coming so soon after the murder of President Kennedy, was made worse by the slaying, two months later in Los Angeles, of the late president's brother, Senator Robert F. Kennedy of New York.

For a time, the lawlessness and violence increased, but eventually emotional reactions were tempered by a realization that not all Americans were murderers, and that continuance of direct-action methods well might end in ruin for all. True, overcrowding, poverty, injustice, "depersonalization," lack of opportunity, careless loss of natural resources, and the continuing drain on men and money in Vietnam were imbuing many with a feeling of despair. But the correcting of these ills, where hundreds of millions of people and centuries of tradition were involved, inevitably was a slow process; it required a willing acceptance by the majority of the basic rights *of all* people, and a full understanding *by all* people of their responsibility to the nation as a whole.

Many of the worst excesses occurred during the middle and late 1960s, and, as customary, blame was heaped upon the incumbent administration. Making the picture even gloomier for President Johnson, was the simultaneous and expanding American involvement in the crisis in Southeast Asia.

After the Japanese occupiers left French Indochina following World War II, France was unable to reestablish her prewar control. The former colonies of Tonkin, Annam, and Cochin-China then came to be known as Vietnam, for which the Geneva Agreements of 1964 provided a temporary division at the seventeenth parallel into Communist-dominated North Vietnam and anti-Communist South Vietnam. As had happened in Korea, this division served as an invitation to the Northern Communists, supported by Moscow and Peking, to harass and eventually try to absorb the South.

To prevent this occurring, and thus to "contain" the Communist area of influence, the United States and several other foreign governments, including South Korea and Thailand, sent troops to help the South. As it had in Korea, so in Vietnam did the United States provide the major share of support. President Eisenhower sent only some military advisers, who did no fighting. But as Communist aid to the North and to South Vietnam Communists increased, first Kennedy and then Johnson sent major ground forces to Southeast Asia. Johnson was the first to commit the ground forces to combat, as he also initiated air operations against selected military targets in the North. By early 1969, when so-called peace talks began in Paris, United States forces in Vietnam numbered more than 540,000. The frustrated military, however, were not permitted by Washington to take all measures necessary to win the war, their charge only was to hammer the Reds into a willingness to negotiate. Thus the American forces were severely handicapped by their own government against an enemy who seemed determined not to let negotiations interfere with outright military victory.

The growing commitment of men and materials had widespread and violent repercussions at home, stimulated largely by pro-Communists, the college youth, liberal intellectuals, and some of the communications media. Johnson was attacked more and more frequently and was accused of having violated his campaign promise of 1964 to avoid entanglement in an Asian war. Many argued that the president in fact was pursuing the very policy that Goldwater had recommended, and as a result of which the Arizonian apparently had lost many votes. The urban violence now became progressively worse, as the pro-Communist and the antiwar Whites joined and, indeed, often spurred the militant Blacks.

Recognizing that these issues would loom large in the next presidential campaign, Johnson in the spring of 1968 announced his decision not to be a candidate for reelection. The Democrats thereupon nominated Vice President Hubert H. Humphrey of Minnesota to oppose the Republican Richard M. Nixon, who had lost to Kennedy in 1960. Governor George C. Wallace of Alabama, a Democrat and at that time an opponent of racial integration, was the candidate of a new third party, the American Independent party. The election was close in terms of popular vote, but Nixon won handily in electoral votes.

In order later to be able to treat as a unit the five years and seven months of Nixon's tenure, let us go at once to the election of 1972. The Republicans renominated President Nixon and Vice President Spiro T. Agnew. The Democratic nomination, after much intraparty maneuvering, went to Senator George S. McGovern of South Dakota and Robert Sargent Shriver, Jr., of New York. Nixon's campaign was based on the value of experience, economic revival, seeming success in a move to end the Vietnam involvement through "peace with honor," and détente with Russia and China. McGovern offered unconditional withdrawal from Southeast Asia, a slashing of defense expenditures, heavier taxation of the well-to-do, and vast appropriations in behalf of the poor. Nixon won a landslide victory, carrying all electoral votes save those of Massachusetts and the District of Columbia. But the Democrats increased their majorities in both houses of Congress.

At the time of Nixon's first inauguration, in January 1969, the United States appeared to be going through a period of unprecedented stress and crisis. Observers were in general agreement that "past assumptions are widely deemed inadequate or irrelevant, traditional concepts and values are being challenged or repudiated, and the fabric of the society is being strained both by group antagonisms and by the widespread rejection of conventional restraints on individual conduct. The basic issue . . . is whether the nation can . . . recover a sense of national purpose that would permit a more effective attack on the pressing problem of racial inequality, urban decay, poverty and malnutrition, rising crime rates, educational deficiencies, environmental pollution and the like."*

One of the early and exhilarating events that occurred during the Nixon administration was the achievement of the United States in placing the first man on the moon. The feat was accomplished by Neil A. Armstrong on July 20, 1969. His deeply felt and never-to-be-forgotten words as he stepped on the surface of this natural satellite of the earth were: "That's one small step for a man, a giant leap for mankind."

In domestic affairs, the president tried to ease national tension by pursuing racial integration more deliberately than had been the case under his predecessor and by striving to check the growing centralization of governmental authority in Washington. Efforts were made, with modest success, to reduce the monstrous welfare burden by the prescription of work obligations for relief payments and by the provision of work-training programs and placement assistance. Poor families with dependent children were given special aid, in part through the use of "food stamps" to make necessities available at a discount. The twenty-sixth Amendment to the Constitution, effective in July, 1971, extended voting rights to citizens from the age of eighteen. In 1972, the Supreme Court declared that the existing state death-penalty laws were unconstitutional because they gave too much discretion and latitude to judges and juries.

American ground troops were withdrawn from combat in Vietnam in August, 1972, and the last United States forces left the wartorn area in March, 1973. Meanwhile, although the machinery of the Selective Service System was retained for future emergency, the draft had been ended at the close of 1972. Nixon visited both Russia and China in 1972. He restored trade and limited diplomatic relations with Peking—at the expense of the previously close relationship between Washington and Taipei, and, in November, 1972, he eliminated the ban on American visits to Red China. Gradually, domestic confidence was restored, the economy improved, unemployment dropped gratifyingly, and, in November, 1972, the Dow-Jones industrial-stocks average rose to the "magic figure" of 1000.

As the months following Nixon's second inauguration, in 1973, wore on, shade fluctuated with light, until the picture became dark. In Vietnam, Henry A. Kissinger, then the president's national security adviser and later the first naturalized citizen to become secretary of state, succeeded in negotiating a ceasefire in January, 1973. Men of good will, especially

---

*Richard P. Stebbins and Alba Amoia, eds., *Political Handbook and Atlas of the World, 1970,* New York, Simon and Schuster for Council on Foreign Relations, 1970, p. 390. Reprinted with permission.

those who really did not comprehend the deviousness of Communist policy, hopefully assumed that the North-South issues now would be settled at a conference table. Instead, Communist North Vietnam and the Vietcong or Reds in South Vietnam stalled, raised artificial obstacles to germane talk, and, in 1974, reopened the war. Early in 1975, Congress denied the president's request for further military aid to the Saigon government in South Vietnam. In April, the Reds took control of all Vietnam.

In the Middle East, Kissinger, though Jewish, managed to arrange an Arab-Israeli disengagement agreement in January, 1974. For some time thereafter he appeared to be drawing Israel and the Arabian states closer to compromise. After more than a year of "air-shuttle diplomacy," however, he gave up in frustration early in 1975, leaving the future of the dispute in the hands of a Geneva Conference, co-chaired by the United States and Russia. Meanwhile, in October, 1973, there had been proclaimed an Arabian oil embargo, used "to pressure" the West, especially the United States, into lessening its support of Israel. Although, again in part through Mr. Kissinger's persuasiveness, the embargo had been lifted in March, 1974, by all the producers save Syria and Libya, the price of crude oil was set by the Arabian rulers at about three times that in 1972.

One result of all this was a serious energy crisis in the West and in Japan. In the United States, the "energy crunch" was all the more severe because of a recent spate of national, state, and local conservation and "anti-pollution" legislation. Much of this was based on the inadequately studied and even unsupported claims of highly vocal professional and amateur "ecologists," who for a time seemed able to exercise almost hypnotic influence over some publicity-seeking legislators. Indeed, one reason for the seriousness of the crisis was the ability of the environmentalists to delay for years the start of work on an Alaskan oil-pipeline. The opening of the Federal Energy Office in late 1973, was of no immediate help, for there appeared to be no agreement among officials on precisely how to alleviate the situation.

The gasoline shortage (though it probably was less critical than some anti-Administration persons in Congress and among the communications media made it out to be) and the industrial antipollution regulations and standards, some of which required the immediate and expensive (though not necessarily wise) correction of procedures that had been legal for generations, combined to stifle the economy and shake public confidence. The automobile industry was hardest hit. Its weakening adversely affected other major industries in chain-reaction form. The dollar was devalued in 1973, and, in October, 1974, the Dow-Jones average, for the first time in twelve years, fell to 600. Rapid inflation—uncustomarily accompanied by a sharp decline in stock prices—rising unemployment, a virtual halt in new-house construction, and lengthy welfare rolls, all helped make the outlook bleak as 1974 drew to a close.

Other happenings, too, upset the public equilibrium. The domestic hijacking of airplanes for ransom or political blackmail reached such grave proportions that Washington, early in 1973, made all airline passengers subject to search before boarding. Although some objected to this "violation" of their "civil rights," the vigorous enforcement of search with increasingly sophisticated electronics equipment virtually eliminated this air piracy.

In 1973, further, a Supreme Court decision in effect legalized abortion by declaring unconstitutional most of the existing state antiabortion laws. Under the Court's ruling, abortion was made permissible during the first trimester of pregnancy. State legislatures might regulate abortion procedures during the second trimester to help safeguard the mother's health. Abortion during the last trimester was declared allowable only in protection of the mother's health and life. This decision, not astonishingly, aroused furor, particularly in Roman Catholic circles. Another Supreme Court decision, this one in 1974, put another sudden economic burden on business, industry, and the professions by ordering at once the same pay for female as for male employees in the same work.

Meanwhile, there had come to light evidence of questionable and illegal acts involving a part of the presidential political family. On October 10, 1973, Vice President Agnew resigned; he pleaded no contest to a charge of income-tax evasion. Under the terms of the twenty-fifth Amendment to the Constitution, effective in 1967, the president was required to nominate a successor. Nixon chose, and the two houses of Congress confirmed, the then Republican House minority leader, Gerald R. Ford of Michigan.

Then evidence appeared that some highly placed individuals in both government and business had violated the law in the fund-raising campaign for the elections of 1972. Beyond this, some energetic Republican campaign aides, seeking material to discredit the Democratic presidential candidate had broken into Democratic headquarters in a Washington apartment building complex named "Watergate." The first guilty pleas in the Watergate affair came during 1973. Soon thereafter, the Senate Investigating Committee summoned for interrogation several of the president's aides.

Rumors were rife that Nixon had become aware of the break-in and had agreed to certain "cover-up" measures. In May, 1974, the president denied knowledge of the cover-up; but then, largely by chance, some recorded tapes were discovered that seemed to indicate his acquiescence in a hushing-up of the crime. In July, on the basis of evidence collected by the Senate Investigating Committee and several special prosecutors, the House voted three Articles of Impeachment against the president. And on August 8, 1974, Nixon resigned.

The enemies, and there were many, whom Nixon and his aides had made during the course of his political life among the communications media and in Congress, were less than fair in their treatment of him, but Nixon himself did not help his case. And in the two years during which "Watergate" almost monopolized the news, he was unable to provide the political leadership that the country sorely needed. Eventually, although he left office under a cloud, all his work in behalf of world peace and the solid domestic achievements of his first administration may be more widely remembered than his missteps.

On August 9, 1974, Vice President Ford was sworn in as president. Expressing the hope that national divisiveness and malaise might thereby be healed, he gave Nixon a full pardon three weeks later, and in September proclaimed a partial amnesty for those who had gone under cover or left the country rather than perform their military service during the war in Southeast Asia. Only a minority of those affected availed themselves of the opportunity to undergo "rehabilitation" through the performance of some designated public or humanitarian service.

It was necessary also for Ford to nominate a new vice president. In September, 1974, he presented to Congress the name of former Governor Nelson A. Rockefeller of New York. Following three months of hearings, and some abusive grilling, the national legislature confirmed the appointment near the close of the year.

*   *   *

In all areas of human activity throughout the world—in government, politics, business, unions, advertising, the communications media, education, private living, and the rest—traditional morality three decades after the end of World War II seemed to be becoming obsolete. Almost it seemed that "deception had been piled on deception until lying—or, at best, distortion and failure to make full disclosure—had become a way of life."* And, everywhere on the globe, humanity at the same time was crying, with Jeremiah, "Peace, peace; when there is no peace." Fortunately for mankind, "hope ever tells us that tomorrow will be better."†

---

*Arthur Hailey, *The Moneychangers,* New York, 1975, p. 369.
†Albius Tibullus, *Elegies,* II, ca. 20 B.C.

WHITE COLLARED SOLDIER

AND IT WAS SUCH A PRETTY PACKAGE

TWO SIDES TO EVERY STORY

THE TRAGEDY OF PANMUNJOM

GODSPEED

"DON'T GET EXCITED—I'LL FIND A WAY!"

—BUT THE MELODY LINGERS ON

NEAR TIME TO WALK ON HIS OWN FEET

THAT INDISPENSABLE TOOL OF AMERICAN FOREIGN POLICY

'REMOVE PLEASE, STRINGS AND LABEL, SENOR!'

'WATCH THAT CAR! NOT SO FAST! TURN RIGHT! STOP! WAIT! SLOW DOWN! ---'

'FOLLOW ME!'

'I DON'T QUITE KNOW WHAT WE SHOULD DO WITH YOU!'

'BUT HE SENT ME OVER HERE!'

'I AGREE TO RETREAT — IN THE CAUSE OF PEACE, OF COURSE!'

MORE THAN THE PRESIDENT'S BLOOD WAS SPILLED

NEWER FRONTIER

'WE'RE RUNNING LOW ON COLD TURKEY, BUT YOU CAN FILL UP ON GRAVY!'

'YOU WOULDN'T THINK THEY'RE SO PRETTY, IF YOU HAD TO RAKE THEM UP!'

NEWS NOTE—
ON PRESIDENTIAL REQUEST, HIGHLY QUALIFIED INDIVIDUALS OF EACH DEPARTMENT AND AGENCY OF GOVERNMENT ARE PREPARING FULL WRITTEN HISTORY OF LBJ ERA.

'… OF LBJ – BY LBJ AND FOR LBJ.'

'WHAT — DIDN'T ANYONE BRING A COMPASS ?'

THERE IS BUT ONE WAY

'HOW DO YOU KNOW HE CAN'T PLAY—YOU DIDN'T EVEN ASK HIM!'

'GIVE ME THE GOOD OLD DAYS WHEN WE WERE KEPT AFTER SCHOOL FOR PLAYING HOOKY!'

'SEE YOU AFTER SCHOOL, TOM — CAN'T MISS MY COMPULSORY BUS!'

ABE LINCOLN'S THIRTY-MILE HIKE TO BORROW A BOOK

SCHOOL BUS

'HE'LL NEVER AMOUNT TO ANYTHING — YOU HAVE TO RIDE A BUS TO GET AN EDUCATION!'

'FOLLOW ME _ WE'LL FIND A WAY OUT _ _ _ I THINK!'

'I WARNED YOU — IF YOU VOTED FOR GOLDWATER, YOU'D VOTE FOR ESCALATION!'

'HE'S ABSOLUTELY RIGHT! WE DO NEED MORE ARMS TO WIN!'

'IF YOU ASK ME, I'D SAY TRY BACKING UP!'

HISTORY LESSON

'YOU'RE LATE! I GUESS YOU'RE GOING TO TELL ME YOU GOT TIED UP!'

'GUESS I FORGOT TO TELL YOU, RICHARD — I'V BEEN MARRIED BEFORE!'

'THINK HE'D GO AWAY–IF I GAVE **HIM** THE CANDY?'

'WHY DON'T YOU RUN ALONG TO BED? YOU WOULDN'T UNDERSTAND THE REST OF IT ANYWAY!'

'I'LL SAY THIS — THEY KEEP US WELL SUPPLIED WITH HEAVY WEAPONS!'

'I MAY DROP OUT THIS SEMESTER, NOTHING MUCH LEFT TO DO BUT STUDY.'

'COULD YOU COME BACK LATER—THE DOCTOR IS TAKING HIS MEDICINE?'

A DWARF ON A GIANT'S SHOULDER, SEES FURTHER OF THE TWO

WHERE THE BLOWS ARE LANDING

'NOW ALL TOGETHER MEN, I SAID ROW NOT ROW!'

287

'YOU DON'T MIND IF I EAT WHILE WE TALK?'

'PSST — MY NEW SECRET WEAPON!'

288

'IT INTERFERES WITH MY GOBBLEDYGOOK!'

'MAO TSE-TUNG? FOLLOW THAT PATH! GOOD LUCK!'

SOVIET AIR POWER

THE SHAPE OF THINGS TO COME

'BRING US TOGETHER AGAIN'

'HOPE YOU DON'T MIND, LEONID! BUT WE'VE HAD TO DISCHARGE SOME OF OUR HELP!'

'HENRY? DON'T UNPACK!'

294

FAMOUS LAST WORDS

'NYET! BOTH!!'

THE BEST LAID SCHEMES O' MICE AND MEN...

'JUST WHEN IT LOOKS LIKE THEY'RE FALLING APART—THEY FALL TOGETHER AGAIN!'

THE UMPIRE'S LOT IS NOT A HAPPY ONE!

'GLAD YOU ASKED ME! YOU'RE THE FIRST POLL TAKER I'VE EVER TALKED TO!'

APPENDIX

The Association of American Editorial Cartoonists (Contributed by Art Wood, Jr.)

Many political cartoonists in public are extrovertish, informed, conversant, erudite, and entertaining. This is the posture before the general public, but what about the relationship with each other, socially and professionally?

While there have been some exceptions to the rule, historically the editorial cartoonist tended to stay apart and to himself. Whether this was the consequence of ego, pressure of work, preference, or the circumstance that there were only one or two of them in a city is debatable. But whatever the reason, a "loner" tendency long predominated.

After World War II, however, a group of editorial cartoonists in the nation's capital decided that it would be helpful, both professionally and socially, to break the traditional stance of aloofness. There would be advantage, they thought, in getting together occasionally for inspiration and fellowship and generally to compare notes.

The founding father of the cartoon "association" idea was a most unlikely looking parent. Back in the 1950s, John Stampone, cartoonist of the *Army Times,* had eternal youth written all over his beaming face. He looked more like a copyboy (which he once was on the *Baltimore Sun*) than a full-fledged widely reprinted nationally known cartoonist. A boyish look and wide grin were his trademark, and his contagious personality had influence far beyond the environs of Washington, D.C., where the *Army Times* office was located.

Stampone was especially close to the Pulitzer prizewinning cartoon team of C. K. and Jim Berryman at the *Washington Star,* and was a good friend of Pulitzer prizewinner Harold Talburt of the Scripps-Howard Newspapers, and of Dan Dowling of the *New York Herald Tribune*. These men formed the nucleus of the group that was to become the Association of American Editorial Cartoonists. Others who contributed time and ideas and helped mold early policy were Roy Justus of the *Minneapolis Star,* Scott Long of the *Minneapolis Tribune,* John Chase of the *New Orleans States-Times,* and Charles Werner of the *Indianapolis Star.*

Actually, it was an article in the *Saturday Review of Literature* that had stimulated Stampone to action by implying that political cartoonists in America were a diminishing force, with little prestige. Stampone, indeed, put great stock in the motto depicted in Benjamin Franklin's first political cartoon, "Join, or Die."

With the help of the *Army Times* publisher, Melvin Ryder, who underwrote expenses for the charter and mailings, Stampone early in 1957 issued an invitation to all the political cartoonists in the United States, as listed in the then current *Editor and Publisher Yearbook,* to join in association. The cartoonists were quick to respond, and eighty of them became charter members of the Association of American Editorial Cartoonists. This first national fraternal group of political cartoonists in the United States was organized at its initial meeting, in Washington, D.C., at the Statler Hotel in May, 1957.

Political speakers at the first convention included Senator Hubert Humphrey of Minnesota, Senator John McClellan of Arkansas, Secretary of Defense Charles Wilson, and the man whom the association elected as an Honorary Member, and who was destined to become perhaps the most caricatured public figure in United States history, the then vice president, Richard M. Nixon.

From this first gathering of cartoonists in the late 1950s, the association has grown to an impressive roster of more than two hundred cartoonists from all over the United States, Canada, and Mexico.

ART WOOD, JR.
Past President